# A Year with Rumi

# A Year with Rumi

*Daily Readings*

༄

## COLEMAN BARKS

With John Moyne, Nevit Ergan, A. J. Arberry,
Reynold Nicolson, and others

HarperOne
*An Imprint of HarperCollinsPublishers*

HarperOne

HarperCollins books may be purchased for educational, business, or sales promotional use. For information, please e-mail the Special Markets Department at SPsales@harpercollins.com.

HarperCollins Web site: http://www.harpercollins.com

HarperCollins®, 📖®, and HarperOne™ are trademarks of HarperCollins Publishers.

Library of Congress Cataloging-in-Publication Data
Barks, Coleman.
A year with Rumi : daily readings / Coleman Barks. — 1st ed.
p. cm.
Based on A. J. Arberry and R. A. Nicholson's translations of Jalal al-Din Rumi's poems and on Nevit Ergin's work from the Turkish and John Moyne's unpublished translations.
Includes index.
ISBN: 978-0-06-084597-1
I. Jalal al-Din Rumi, Maulana, 1207-1273.   II. Nicholson, Reynold Alleyne, 1868-1945.   III. Arberry, A. J. (Arthur John), 1905-1969.   IV. Title.
PS3552.A671743   2006
891'.5511—dc22                                        2005055149

20  LSC(H)  30  29  28  27  26  25  24  23  22  21

# CONTENTS

# INTRODUCTION

## THE LOVE RELIGION, WILD SOULBOOKS, AND WHAT IS

The story of Rumi's life is well known. Born in the early thirteenth century into a lineage of scholars and mystics in Balkh (then at the eastern edge of the Persian empire, now in northern Afghanistan), he left as a boy with his family just ahead of the advancing armies of Genghis Khan. After several years of traveling they settled in Konya (south-central Turkey), where Rumi became the leader, after his father Bahauddin's death, of a dervish learning community. His life and consciousness changed radically after the meeting in 1244 with his teacher and friend, Shams Tabriz, a wandering meditator of fiery force and originality. The inner work that Shams did with Rumi and Rumi with Shams produced the poetry. It springs from their friendship.

The words that came so spontaneously carry a broad range of religious awareness: the meditative silence and *no-mind* of Zen, the open heart and compassion of Jesus, the stern discipline of Muhammad, the convivial humor of Taoists, the crazy wisdom and bright intelligence of the Jewish Hassidic masters. Rumi is a planetary poet, loved the world over for the grandeur of his surrender and for the freedom and grace of his poetry. He was nurtured within the Islamic tradition, the Persian language, and a long line of Sufis, but it is his connection with Shams of Tabriz that lets his work transcend definition and doctrine. The poetry feels as though it belongs to all. When he died in 1273, members of every religion came to the funeral. Wherever you stand, his words deepen your connection to the mystery of being alive.

The wide use of Rumi texts in multicultural gatherings, that vivid and characterizing feature of our landscape, has roots, I believe, in the continuous human search for true identity, for soul. Whatever the soul is, it does get fed by practices that honor its presence. Such practices might include walking for a lot of people in these sedentary times, and also the habit of reading a wild soulbook. Those volumes vary with each taste and need. Montaigne's *Essays* for Emerson, Rousseau for Hazlitt, Turgenev's *A Sportsman's Sketches* for Hemingway, Chekhov for Raymond Carver. Dickens for Faulkner. Taoist poetry for Robert Bly. G. K. Chesterton for Andrew Dick. Benedetto Croce for Rabindranath Tagore. Nietzsche for Edwin Muir, Flann O'Brien's *The Third Policeman* for John Seawright. D. H. Lawrence's poetry for Galway Kinnell, P. G. Wodehouse for Robert West, Goethe's *Letters to Eckermann* for my sister Betsy (Elizabeth Cox), Henri Nouwen for my brother Herb, Meister Eckhart for James Wright, *Lord Jim* for Annie Dillard, Thornton Wilder for Ed Hicks, Ruskin and Crabb Robinson for Mary Oliver, Ibn Arabi for Ed Hirsch. Mark's Gospel and Hardy's poetry for Donald Hall. Euripides for C. S. Lewis, *Hamlet* and *King Lear* for Ellen Williams. For Elizabeth Bishop it was a rocklike, very dull *second* volume of a study on some industrial technique, for Marianne Moore, a Saturday morning lecture on Java. I wonder what would be a wild soulbook for Harry Crews. James Agee? For me, since 1976, I have felt the bright wind coming from Rumi. *The Shams* and *The Masnavi*.[1]

I devised a soulbook practice for myself that eventually became this Rumi work and play. After a day of teaching sophomore literature at a university—this was in September 1976—I would walk to the Bluebird Restaurant, have some hot tea, mull an oceanic page or two of Arberry's translations, and rephrase a section into a free-verse poem with a title. I was trying to reenter the trance of the poem and get the feel of its creative freedom. Rumi has not been my only soulbook these last thirty years. There's also García Márquez, Colin Wilson, Cormac McCarthy, Ryokan, Edwin Muir, Henry Miller, James Dickey, Gary Snyder, Whitman, and Charlie Smith's poetry. This year it is bird callings, and I refuse to explain.

Roy Ashley taught us this Emily Dickinson in high school.

Some keep the Sabbath going to Church—
I keep it, staying at Home—
With a Bobolink for a Chorister—
And an Orchard, for a Dome.

Some keep the Sabbath in Surplice—
I, just wear my Wings—
And instead of tolling the bell, for Church,
Our little Sexton—sings.
God preaches, a noted Clergyman—

And the sermon is never long,
So instead of getting to Heaven, at last—
I'm going, all along.

Roy's voice had the conviction of Emily's truth because he lived it, keeping not only the Sabbath but every late afternoon in a sacred solitude, walking and bird-whistling his spontaneous compositions, going along as he did. I grew up on the campus of a boys' boarding school where my father was headmaster. Mr. Ashley lived in an apartment near ours and would stroll his whistling past our screen porch. Unselfconscious, virtuoso, operatic, impersonal, poignant—I have never heard anything like that trilling. People used to whistle in public more than they do now. Roy Ashley seemed not to claim his music, and only rarely did anyone speak of it, never to interrupt. That strange, uncommon human birdsong was a teaching whole unto itself. Thomas Mann was his soulbook genius, I think: *The Magic Mountain* and *Buddenbrooks*.

The same year that I first heard Emily's call to churchlessness, 1952, I heard another call too. The Billy Graham Crusade came to town and I went up front for the invitation. Under the sweet counsel of a man named Chuck Bovee, I began a program of memorizing Bible verses, two hundred and twenty-seven of them, all from the King James. It was a profound love for a soulbook, the New Testament. *Les Misérables* and *The Return of the Native* were other soulbooks for me then, at fifteen. I carried whatever group of twenty-five New Testament verses I was working on in a black leather packet in my back pocket. One day when I was scuffling with my archrival, Billy D. Pettway, the verse wallet fell to the ground. He picked it up. What's this? Rubbers? There was no explanation for the weird spirit-longing leap I had taken. "Bible verses I'm memorizing," said I in dismay.

Now I have made a pack of poetry lines for my teenage grand-daughter Briny. Shakespeare, Blake, Dickinson, Mary Oliver, Keats, Galway Kinnell, Mark Twain. For this open-air sanctuary that a lot of us live in, without buildings, or doctrine, or clergy, without *silsila* (lineage), or hierarchy, in an experiment to live not so much *without* religion as *in friendship* with all three hundred of them, and all literatures too. It is a brave try for openness and fresh inspiration.[2]

It is what sent Whitman out walking around Brooklyn. His mother said, He goes out and he comes back in; that's all he does. It is what prompted Thoreau's rambling retreat to Walden Pond. It is Huck floating on the river at night. Melville looks out his study window in the Berkshires and writes the ocean of *Moby Dick*. Jake Barnes in Hemingway's *The Sun Also Rises* slips into an old Spanish church to listen to his thoughts. Wallace Stevens speaks from inside the intensest rendezvous, where God and the imagination are one. Joseph Campbell follows his bliss, researching myth and symbol in the New York Public Library. Gary Snyder works on an ax handle in the high Sierra. Annie Dillard stares down into Tinker Creek. REM's Michael Stipe stands on stage, *Losing my religion*. Iris DeMent suggests that we *Let the mystery be*. All are participating in this global amateur production. We are lucky to have so many luminous figures in this country, but this lineage is not *American*. It comes down through such varied innumerable strands that it cannot be called a lineage at all.

The records of wandering kept by Basho, Cervantes, Homer, and Allan Ginsberg. Mary Oliver's faithful early morning walks with a rainproof surveyor's notebook in her hip pocket. John Muir and Audubon. Anyone who heads out to see what happens, just to enjoy the trip. Needn't go far, needn't leave town. Rumi says that merely being in a body and sentient is a state of pure rapture. Form is ecstatic. Those who know that are the ones I'm talking about, and to. Those photographers who love wilderness and the depths of a human face. The radiant noticing of animals that shows in the cave drawings. It comes through Van Gogh and Cezanne, the way they saw splendor transpiring through what appears. Dutch light. Through Blake. All religions are one, saith Willy, and energy is eternal delight. Hopkins. It comes through south India and the Sufis. Indigenous rock art, Tibet. Hieronymous Bosch and Brueghel, Lao Tzu and Chuang Tzu. Bodhidharma, Rinzai, and that homely flower Mahakashyap was handed by his friend Gautama. That theology-flower of suchness might be a logo for it. No, no names. No flag. Dreamtime drawings. Chekhov's holy chuckle, Dostoyevsky's vivid seekers. The great Greeks and their love of impossible human conversation. Socrates and Plato are saints in this tradition. Saint Francis and my grandson Tuck, too, he will be surprised to know. All children. Gurdjieff. Ramakrishna. Camus and Beckett. Plotinus. Nietzsche prancing naked. And watch as it widens out so beautifully in Galway Kinnell's "Prayer":

*Whatever happens. Whatever*
*what is is is what*
*I want. Only that. But that.*

It is joyfully scientific, this pared-down, vast, three-*ises*-in-a-row petition of Galway's. The world is so amazingly interesting, I want to be completely here for its moment. That longing is the truth I try to follow, rather than a religion's iconography. Watch an astronomer or a molecular biologist at work, an estuarist opening the net he has pulled up out of Doboy Sound. They *glow* as the facts of the world surface. I have found in my experience that good scientists and good mystics are natural friends, good carpenters too. Chefs and surgeons, historians, athletes, all so full of wonder, lovingly careful, and living right at the point of contact, the nailhead of attention and spontaneity.

Saint Teresa stirring the soup, Dan Patterson receiving Sister Miriam's Shaker gift song. Einstein said that science has totally failed to demystify the universe, now that matter does not exist anymore. Sticks and stones are both made of energy, like love and language. Eddington says the universe is less like a thing than it is like a thought.

If this scruffy, thoughtful, ecstatic crowd needs a name, call them the DUMs, the Disreputable Unaffiliated Mystics, though most are not at all disreputable, and many are devoutly affiliated. Vitalists. Advocates of a perennial philosophy. Pan-somethings or other. Whatever you dub these bright beings, they recognize one another across centuries and cultures. Best not to call them anything. Someone might try to organize them and ruin the fun. The broad interest now in the boundary-dissolving poetry of Rumi is evidence of health in this rebellious, but always kind, impulse.

If blasphemy is possible in this experiment to know and live *what is,* perhaps it is in *whatever insults the soul.* Whitman tells us to dismiss such things. But what are those insults? Some come from within. Boredom, cruelty, a cold unresponsiveness, a self-absorbed shyness, depression, addiction. Some from without. War by concept, the insane greed of empire, marketing sterilization and bourgeois dumbing-down. Does the exclusivity of the Abrahamic religious doctrines qualify? The ONLY begotten, the CHOSEN people, the LAST prophet. I would say yes, they do, agreeing with the Sufi Sarmad, who refused to recite the part of the Islamic creed that held that there was but *one* messenger, *one* book, *one* revelation (theirs, of course). Sarmad felt that the whole of creation was sacred, and he sensed that there had been, and will be, many valid ways of acknowledging mystery. His beheaded head died saying that. The exclusive-doctrine people got him.

So whatever keeps the soul from moving along (motion and shapeshifting are great nourishers of soul), whatever keeps it from traveling, from expanding and deepening in love, and living the truth of expressing that, those are the "insults" we need to be alert for.

A Roy Ashley story from further back, 1947. Tony Heywood and I are ten, with BB guns. We decide one morning to stalk and kill something, anything really. A big blue jay. The BB guns are so weak, we could probably have *thrown* a BB to more effect. We stalk and shoot and chase his blue beleaguered noisy self all around that hill's trees, until Mr. Ashley sees what we are up to, comes down to the clearing behind the baseball backstop, and puts a stern and sudden end to our stupid cruelty. I still feel the sting of that remorse as we came back to our normal tenderheartedness after such forgetting. The present Dalai Lama says, *Kindness is my religion*. Whatever the soul is, it truly does love kindness where it finds it, in text or tree or teacher. So say soul is a friend, a weather and a master, the deep being within each that can somehow be met, talked with, lived and fallen into as we let go the mind, or find a soulbook to flee with into its wide-open companionable space. Reading is flight school, Himalayan cave, and possibly a meeting with an unimaginable teacher and friend like Shams Tabriz. That is a lot to claim for reading. It might be just as true to say that reading is a way of avoiding that deepening. But I would rather anticipate that this three-inch persimmon seedling in the bucket of potting soil behind my house will eventually grow to eighty feet. Some have. Jelaluddin Chelabi, head of the Mevlevi order of dervishes (the ones descended from Rumi), once asked me, What religion are you? I gave him the arms-open, palms-up *who-knows* gesture. Good, he said. Love is the religion, and the universe is the book.

Here is how Ibn Arabi speaks of the all-inclusive, no-dogma, no-structure way. The light at the end of this poem is both subject and subjectivity.

### The Love Religion

The inner space inside
that we call the heart
has become many different
living scenes and stories.

A pasture for sleek gazelles,
a monastery for Christian monks,
a temple with Shiva dancing,
a kaaba for pilgrimage.

The tablets of Moses are there,
the Qur'an, the Vedas,
the sutras, and the gospels.

Love is the religion in me.
Whichever way love's camel goes,
that way becomes my faith,
the source of beauty, and a light
of sacredness over everything.

# NOTES

1. The A. J. Arberry translations were first: *Mystical Poems of Rumi* (Persian Heritage Series No. 3, University of Chicago Press, 1968) and *Mystical Poems of Rumi* (Persian Heritage Series No. 23, Westview Press, Boulder, CO, 1979). Then the three volumes of Reynold Nicholson's translation of *The Masnavi* with their Commentaries: *The Mathnawi of Jalalu'ddin Rum* (Luzac, London, 1925–40). Also the work of Nevit Ergin and M. G. Gupta, and of course, the collaboration with John Moyne. See the References headnote.

2. I am not opposed to churches. There is a deep human value in the rituals they provide. I love to enter the sacred space of a church, and also that of a mosque, a synagogue, a Hindu temple, the space described by standing stones, and the high mountain retreats of Bhutan. The singing and the friendships found in these communities can be very beautiful. It is just that the turf-squabbling of the organized religions has become hazardous to the health of a wider community and maybe to that of the planet itself.

# JANUARY

### A Just-Finishing Candle

A candle is made to become entirely flame.
In that annihilating moment
it has no shadow.

It is nothing but a tongue of light
describing a refuge.

Look at this
just-finishing candle stub
as someone who is finally safe
from virtue and vice,

the pride and the shame
we claim from those.

## A Single Brushstroke Down

Light dawns, and any talk of *proof*
resembles a blind man's cane at sunrise.

Remember the passage,
*We are with you wherever you are.*

Come back to that.
When did we ever leave it?

No matter we're in a prison of forgetting
or enjoying the banquet of wisdom,
we are always inside presence.

Drunkenly asleep, tenderly awake,
clouded with grief, laughing like lightning,
angry at war, quiet with gratitude, we are nothing
in this many-mooded world of weather
but a single brushstroke down,
speaking of presence.

*The word* Allah *in Arabic begins with a strong
downward mark.*

### Children Running Through

I used to be shy.
You made me sing.

I used to refuse things at table.
Now I shout for more wine.

In somber dignity, I used to sit
on my mat and pray.

Now children run through
and make faces at me.

## *The Elegance of the Ermine*

Midnight, and a messenger comes from a prayer niche,
someone as quiet as moonlight,
yet with a torch that burns our sleeping.

A king knocks on the doorkeeper's door
and laughing, leads everyone out to a table.

Our lips tremble at the cup, with the same trembling
as a drop of mercury.

The gentleness of the host is the same
as that that made the elegance of the ermine.

The dry and wet of a love affair,
those tears are identical to the taking in
and giving away of a waterwheel's turning.

The keys that open all gates
are strapped to love's chest.

When a bird is completely broken and still,
it gets removed from the snare.

This list of rude likenesses
does not come near saying
what happens in our lives.

## *Birdwings*

Your grief for what you've lost lifts a mirror
up to where you're bravely working.

Expecting the worst, you look, and instead,
here's the joyful face you've been wanting to see.

Your hand opens and closes and opens and closes.
If it were always a fist or always stretched open,
you would be paralyzed.

Your deepest presence
is in every small contracting and expanding,
the two as beautifully balanced and coordinated
as birdwings.

*Sometimes I Do*

In your light I learn how to love.
In your beauty, how to make poems.

You dance inside my chest,
where no one sees you,

but sometimes I do,
and that light becomes this art.

*Don't Let Your Throat Tighten*

Don't let your throat tighten
with fear. Take sips of breath
all day and night, before death
closes your mouth.

### *There Is Something in Us*

Imagine a man selling his donkey
to be with Jesus.

Now imagine him selling Jesus
to get a ride on a donkey.
This does happen.

Jesus can transform a drunk into gold.
If the drunk is already golden,
he can be changed to pure diamond.
If already that, he can become the circling
planets, Jupiter, Venus, the moon.

Never think that you are worthless.
God has paid an enormous amount for you,
and the gifts keep arriving.

There is something in us
that has nothing to do with night and day,
grapes that never saw a vineyard.

WE ARE ALL RETURNING

says the Qur'an. Enjoy Shams,
or if you cannot do that, at least
consider what honest people tell you.

# JANUARY 9

---

### *Gnats Inside the Wind*

Some gnats come from the grass to speak with Solomon.

O Solomon, you are the champion of the oppressed.
You give justice to the little guys, and they don't get
any littler than us. We are tiny metaphors
for frailty. Can you defend us?

Who has mistreated you?

Our complaint is against the wind.

Well, says Solomon, you have pretty voices,
you gnats, but remember, a judge cannot listen
to just one side. I must hear both litigants.

Of course, agree the gnats.

Summon the East Wind, calls out Solomon,
and the wind arrives almost immediately.

What happened to the gnat plaintiffs? Gone.

Such is the way of every seeker who comes to complain
at the High Court. When the presence of God arrives,
where are the seekers? First there's dying,
then union, like gnats inside the wind.

### A Piece of Wood

I reach for a piece of wood. It turns into a lute.
I do some meanness. It turns out helpful.
I say one must not travel during the holy month.
Then I start out, and wonderful things happen.

### *Backpain*

Muhammad went to visit a sick friend.
Such kindness brings more kindness,
and there is no knowing the proliferation from there.

The man was about to die.
Muhammad put his face close and kissed him.

His friend began to revive.
Muhammad's visit re-created him.
He began to feel grateful for an illness
that brought such light.

And also for the backpain
that wakes him in the night.

No need to snore away like a buffalo
when this wonder is walking the world.

There are values in pain that are difficult
to see without the presence of a guest.

Don't complain about autumn.
Walk with grief like a good friend.
Listen to what he says.

Sometimes the cold and dark of a cave
give the opening we most want.

### *The Night Ocean*

We are the the night ocean filled
with glints of light. We are the space
between the fish and the moon,
while we sit here together.

### *The Gift of Water*

Someone who does not know the Tigris River exists
brings the caliph who lives near the river
a jar of fresh water. The caliph accepts, thanks him,
and gives in return a jar filled with gold coins.

Since this man has come through the desert,
he should return by water. Taken out by another door,
the man steps into a waiting boat and sees
the wide freshwater of the Tigris. He bows his head,
What wonderful kindness that he took my gift.

Every object and being in the universe is a jar
overfilled with wisdom and beauty, a drop of the Tigris
that cannot be contained by any skin. Every jarful
spills and makes the earth more shining,
as though covered in satin.

If the man had seen even a tributary of the great river,
he would not have brought the innocence of his gift.
Those that stay and live by the Tigris grow so ecstatic
that they throw rocks at the jugs, and the jugs
become perfect. They shatter. The pieces dance,
and water . . . Do you see?

Neither jar nor water nor stone, nothing.
You knock at the door of reality, shake
your thought-wings, loosen your shoulders, and open.

## The Mill

The heart is a wheatgrain. We are the mill
where this body is a millstone
and thought, the moving river.

The body asks the river why it runs on so.
The river says, Ask the miller who made
the millrace that directs my falling
that turns your stone.

The miller says, You that love bread,
if this turning were not happening,
what would you dip in your broth?

So a lot of questioning goes on
around the milling of wheat,
but what really *is* this breadmaking work?

Now let silence ask
about wheat and the river,
about the miller and the stone
and the taste of bread dipped in soup,
and this listening we do at the mill.

*The mill is one of Rumi's images for the process whereby
individual grains get crushed to make something less sepa-
rate, more communally useful (bread). Thought (the riverwa-
ter) and the body (the millstone) are part of this work, as are
the miller (creative intelligence) and the customer (desire),
who wants a piece of bread for his soup.*

# JANUARY 15

## *Bu'l-Hasan and the Snow*

After Bestami died, it happened as he said
that Bu'l-Hasan became the sheikh for his community.

Every day Bu'l-Hasan would go to Bestami's tomb
to receive instruction. He had been told to do this
in a dream by Bestami himself.

Every dawn he goes and stands
facing the tomb until midmorning.

Either the spirit of Bestami comes and talks to him
or in silence the questions he has are answered.

One day a deep snow has fallen overnight.
The graves are indistinguishable.
Bu'l-Hasan feels lost.

Then he hears his sheikh's voice.
The world is made of snow.
It falls and melts and falls again.

Do not be concerned with the snow.
Come toward the sound of my voice.
Move always in this direction.

From that day Bu'l-Hasan began to experience
the enlightened state
he had only heard and read about before.

# JANUARY 16

*Let the Beauty We Love*

Today, like every other day, we wake up empty
and frightened. Don't open the door to the study
and begin reading. Take down a musical instrument.

Let the beauty we love be what we do.
There are hundreds of ways to kneel and kiss the ground.

## *Love Moves Away*

Pale sunlight,
pale the wall.

Love moves away.
The light changes.

I need more grace
than I thought.

### The Old Woman and the Falcon

When you give a noble falcon
to a fussy old woman who knows nothing of falconry,
she will clip its wings short, *for its own good.*

Young man, where has your mother been
that your toenails have gotten this long?
Those talons are how the falcon hunts its food.

The old woman fixes him *tutmaj,* dumpling stew.
He won't touch it. Too good to eat my *tutmaj,* huh?
She ladles some broth and holds it to his beak.
Her anger builds, and suddenly she pours
the ladle of hot soup over his head.

Tears come from those beautiful falcon eyes.
He remembers his former life, the king's love-whistle,
the great circling over the ocean,
the distances that condense so quickly to a point.

Falcon tears are food for a true human being,
perfume for Gabriel.

Your soul is the king's falcon,
who says, *This old woman's rage
does not touch my glory or my discipline.*

### Hallaj

Hallaj said what he said and went to the origin
through the hole in the scaffold.
I cut a cap's worth of cloth from his robe,
and it swamped over me from head to foot.
Years ago, I broke a bunch of roses
from the top of his wall. A thorn from that
is still in my palm, working deeper.
A person comes to him naked. It's cold.
There's a fur coat floating in the river.
Jump in and get it, he says.
You dive in. You reach for the coat.
It reaches for you.
It's a live bear that has fallen in upstream,
drifting with the current.
How long does it take? Hallaj yells from the bank.
Don't wait, you answer. This coat
has decided to wear me home.

A little part of a story, a hint.
Do you need long sermons on Hallaj?

### *The Sunrise Ruby*

In the early morning hour,
just before dawn, lover and beloved wake
and take a drink of water.

She asks, Do you love me or yourself more?
Really, tell the absolute truth.

He says, There is nothing left of me.
I am like a ruby held up to the sunrise.
Is it still a stone, or a world
made of redness? It has no resistance
to sunlight. The ruby and the sunrise are one.
Be courageous and discipline yourself.

Work. Keep digging your well.
Don't think about getting off from work.
Submit to a daily practice.
Your loyalty to that is a ring on the door.

Keep knocking, and the joy inside
will eventually open a window
and look out to see who's there.

## *A Night Full of Talking*

A night full of talking that hurts,
my worst held-back secrets. Everything
has to do with loving and not loving.
This night will pass.
Then we have work to do.

### The Price of Kissing

I would love to kiss you.
*The price of kissing is your life.*

Now my loving is running toward my life shouting,
*What a bargain, let's buy it.*

*Farther and Farther from Zero*

Suddenly, I fall from the pavilion
into a place where I see the ugliness,
hypocrisy, rouge on a sunken face,
a thorn lodged in a kidney, the blind crone
holding a laurel wreath for the winner,
her black ribbons in shreds,
her eyes dark wth purple,
a gold anklet on her shriveled leg.

The puppet show looks charming,
but go behind the screen and see who runs it.

Wash your hands and face of this charade.
Anyone who wants these prizes
flares up quickly like a wood chip.

There is one who can help,
who turns the wheel from nonexistence
to a sweet-breathing emptiness.

Words are ways we add up breath,
counting stress and syllable
with our exacting musical knack
that takes us farther and farther from zero.

## *The Visions of Daquqi (1)*

Husam, tell about the visions of Daquqi,
who said, I have traveled east and west
not knowing which way I was going,
following the moon, lost inside God.

Someone asked, Why do you go barefooted
over the stones and thorns.

What, he answered. What.

A bewildered lover does not walk on feet.
He or she walks on love. There are no "long"
or "short" trips for those. No time.

The body learned from spirit how to travel.
A saint's body moves in the unconditioned way,
though it seems to be in conditionedness.

Daquqi said, One day I was going along
looking to see in people the shining of the Friend.
I came to the shore at twilight and saw
seven candles. I hurried along the beach
toward them. I was amazed. My amazement was amazed.
Waves of bewilderment broke over my head.

*The Visions of Daquqi (2)*

What are those candles that no one seems to see?
In the presence of such lights
people were looking for lamps to buy.

Then the seven became one,
in the middle of the sky's rim.
Then that fanned out to seven again.

There were connections between the candles
that cannot be said. I saw, but I cannot say.
They became seven men and then seven trees,
so dense with leaves and fruit no limbs were visible.

Flashes of light
spurted from each fruit like juice.

And most marvelous of all was that hundreds
of thousands of people were passing beside the trees,
risking their lives, sacrificing everything,
to find some scrap of shade. No one saw
the trees with their tremendous shade.

## The Visions of Daquqi (3)

The caravans had no food, yet food was dropping
all about them. If someone had said,
*Look, over here*, they would have thought him insane.

How can this happen. Am I dreaming?
I walk up to the trees. I eat the fruit.
I may as well believe.

Then the seven trees become one and then seven again.
At every second they are both one and seven.
Then they are seven men seated in meditation
for the sake of the one reality.

I come closer and wave. They call,
O Daquqi, the glory and the crown.

How do they know my name?
They have never seen me until now.
Immediately they know my thought
and smile at each other.

Honored one, is this still hidden from you?
How can anything be hidden from one so dissolved in God?
I think inwardly, If this is the spirit-reality,
how is it we are speaking words and saying names?

---

### *The Visions of Daquqi (4)*

One of the seven answers, Names, sometimes
the names slip away,
but it is not forgetfulness.
It is our being so absorbed.

Then they all say to me,
Would you lead us in prayer?

Yes. But wait awhile.
I am still in some temporal confusion
that will be solved by companionship with you.

Through companionship with the ground
a grapevine grows. It opens
into the earth's darkness and flies.

It becomes selfless in the presence
of its origin and learns what it really is.

They nod, as though to say, Whenever you are ready.
That nodding was a flame in my heart.
I was freed from hourly time,
from sequence and relation.

## *The Many Wines*

God has given us a dark wine so potent
that, drinking it, we leave the two worlds.

God made Majnun love Layla so much
that just her dog would cause confusion in him.

There are thousands of wines
that can take over our minds.

Don't think all ecstasies are the same.
Jesus was lost in his love for God.
His donkey was drunk with barley.

Every object, every being,
is a jar full of delight.
Be a connoiseur, and taste with caution.

Any wine will get you high.
Judge like a king, and choose the purest,
not the ones adulterated with fear,
or some urgency about "what's needed."

Drink the wine that moves you
as a camel moves when it's been untied,
and is just ambling about.

### Uthman's Silence

The story is told of Uthman, who when he became caliph
mounted quickly the steps of Muhammad's pulpit,
whereas Abu Bakr, out of respect for the prophet,
seated himself on the second step.

There were three steps. Omar sat on the third step.
Uthman climbed to the top. When asked why, he replied,
If I sat on the third step, people would say
I was like Omar. If on the second step,
*He's like Abu Bakr.*

But up here where the chosen one sat, no one will think
to compare *me* with that king of the spirit.

And sometimes when he had climbed
to the preaching place, that sweet one Uthman,
would not say anything. He stayed silent
until midafternoon. No one asked him
for a sermon, and no one left the mosque.

In the silence many began to see with Uthman's light.
This is how a living master opens the inner eye.

## A Dumb Experiment

Break open your personal self
to taste the story of the nutmeat soul.

These voices come from that rattling
against the outer shell.

The nut and the oil inside
have voices that can only be heard
with another kind of listening.

If it weren't for the sweetness of the nut,
the inner talking, who would ever shake a walnut?

We listen to words
so we can silently
reach into the other.

Let the ear and mouth get quiet,
so this taste can come to the lip.

Too long we have been saying poetry,
talking discourses, explaining the mystery outloud.

Let us try a dumb experiment.

## *Two Kinds of Intelligence*

There are two kinds of intelligence: one acquired,
as a child in school memorizes facts and concepts
from books and from what the teacher says,
collecting information from the traditional sciences
as well as from the new sciences.

With such intelligence you rise in the world.
You get ranked ahead or behind others
in regard to your competence in retaining
information. You stroll with this intelligence
in and out of fields of knowledge, getting always
more marks on your preserving tablets.

There is another kind of tablet, one
already completed and preserved inside you.
A spring overflowing its springbox. A freshness
in the center of the chest. This other intelligence
does not turn yellow or stagnate. It's fluid,
and it does not move from outside to inside
through the conduits of plumbing-learning.

This second knowing is a fountainhead
from within you, moving out.

# FEBRUARY

## As Much as a Pen Knows

Do you think that I know what I'm doing?
That for one breath or half-breath I belong to myself?

As much as a pen knows what it's writing,
or the ball can guess where it's going next.

## *Lightning*

This is no ordinary friendship.
I attend your banquet as wine attends.

Like lightning, I am an expert at dying.
Like lightning, this beauty has no language.

It makes no difference
whether I win or lose.

You sit with us in a congregation of the dead,
where one handful of dirt says,
I was once a head of hair.

Another, I was a backbone.
You say nothing.

Love comes in, I can deliver you
from yourself in *this* moment.

Now lover and beloved grow quiet.
My mouth is burning with sweetness.

*The Freshness*

When it's cold and raining,
you are more beautiful.

And the snow brings me
even closer to your lips.

The inner secret, that which was never born,
you are that freshness, and I am with you now.

I can't explain the goings,
or the comings. You enter suddenly,

and I am nowhere again.
Inside the majesty.

### *Someone Digging in the Ground*

An eye is meant to see things.
The soul is here for its own joy.
A head has one use: for loving a true love.
Legs: to run after.

Love is for vanishing into the sky. The mind,
for learning what men have done and tried to do.
Mysteries are not to be solved. The eye goes blind
when it only wants to see *why*.

A lover is always accused of something.
But when he finds his love, whatever was lost
in the looking comes back completely changed.

On the way to Mecca, many dangers: thieves,
the blowing sand, only camel's milk to drink.

Still, each pilgrim kisses the black stone there
with pure longing, feeling in the surface
the taste of the lips he wants.

This talk is like stamping new coins. They pile up,
while the real work is being done outside
by someone digging in the ground.

*Throat-Song*

Let your throat-song
be clear and strong enough

to make an emperor fall full-length,
suppliant, at the door.

## *Unfold Your Own Myth*

Who gets up early to discover the moment light begins?
Who finds us here circling, bewildered, like atoms?
Who, like Jacob blind with grief and age,
smells the shirt of his lost son
and can see again?
Who lets a bucket down and brings up
a flowing prophet? Or like Moses goes for fire
and finds what burns inside the sunrise?

Jesus slips into a house to escape enemies,
and opens a door to the other world.
Solomon cuts open a fish, and there's a gold ring.
Omar storms in to kill the prophet
and leaves with blessings.

But don't be satisfied with stories, how things
have gone with others. Unfold
your own myth, so everyone will understand
the passage, *We have opened you.*

Start walking toward Shams. Your legs will get heavy
and tired. Then comes a moment of feeling
the wings you've grown, lifting.

*I Honor Those*

I honor those who try
to rid themselves of any lying,
who empty the self
and have only clear being there.

### A Pilgrimage to a Person

When you are not with close friends,
you are not in the presence.

It is sad to leave the people you travel with.
How much moreso those who remind you of God.
Hurry back to the ones protecting you.

On every trip, have only one objective,
to meet those who are friends
inside the presence.

If you stay home, keep the same purpose,
to meet the innermost presence
as it lives in people.

Be a pilgrim to the kaaba inside a human being,
and Mecca will rise into view on its own.

### The One Thing You Must Do

There is one thing in this world which you must never forget to do. If you forget everything else and not this, there is nothing to worry about, but if you remember everything else and forget this, then you will have done nothing in your life.

It is as if a king has sent you to some country to do a task, and you perform a hundred other services, but not the one he sent you to do. So human beings come to this world to do *particular work*. That work is the purpose, and each is specific to the person. If you don't do it, it's as though a knife of the finest tempering were nailed into a wall to hang things on. For a penny an iron nail could be bought to serve for that.

Remember the deep root of your being, the presence of your lord. Give your life to the one who already owns your breath and your moments. If you don't, you will be like the one who takes a precious dagger and hammers it into his kitchen wall for a peg to hold his dipper gourd. You will be wasting valuable keeness and foolishly ignoring your dignity and your purpose.

## Water and the Moon

There is a path from me to you
that I am constantly looking for,

so I try to keep clear and still
as water does with the moon.

## *The Water You Want*

**Someone may be clairvoyant, able to see**
the future, and yet have very little wisdom.

Like the man who saw water in his dream,
and began leading everyone toward the mirage.

I am the one with heart-vision.
I have torn open the veil.

**So they set out with him inside the dream,**
while he is actually sleeping
beside a river of pure water.

Any search moves away from the spot
where the object of the quest is.

Sleep deeply wherever you are on the way.
Maybe some traveler will wake you.

Give up subtle thinking, the twofold, threefold
multiplication of mistakes.

Listen to the sound of waves within you.

You are dreaming your thirst,
when the water you want
is inside the big vein on your neck.

### *Evolutionary Intelligence*

This groggy time we live, this is what it is like:
A man goes to sleep in the town
where he has always lived, and he dreams
he is living in another town.
He believes the reality of the dream town.

The world is that kind of sleep.
The dust of many crumbled cities
settles over us like a forgetful doze,
but we are older than those cities.

We began as a mineral. We emerged into plant life
and into the animal state. Then into being human,
and always we have forgotten our former states,
except in early spring when we almost
remember being green again.

Humankind is being led along an evolving course,
through this migration of intelligences,
and though we seem to be sleeping,
there is an inner wakefulness that directs the dream.

It will eventually startle us back
to the truth of who we are.

### *Escaping to the Forest*

Some souls have gotten free of their bodies.
Do you see them? Open your eyes for those
who escape to meet with other escapees,
whose hearts associate in a way they have
of leaving their false selves
to live in a truer self.

I don't mind if my companions
wander away for a while.

They will come back like a smiling drunk.
Thirsty ones die of their thirst.

A nightingale sometimes
flies from a garden
to sing in the forest.

*Love's Confusing Joy*

If you want what visible reality
can give, you are an employee.

If you want the unseen world,
you are not living with your truth.

Both wishes are foolish,
but you'll be forgiven for forgetting
that what you really want is
love's confusing joy.

### *Whoever's Calm and Sensible*

There is a light seed grain inside.
You fill it with yourself, or it dies.

I'm caught in this curling energy. Your hair.
Whoever's calm and sensible is insane.

### The Seed Market

Can you find another market like this?
Where, with your one rose
you can buy hundreds of rose gardens?

Where, for one seed you get a whole wilderness?
For one weak breath, the divine wind?

You have been fearful of being absorbed
in the ground, or drawn up by the air.

Now your waterbead lets go
and drops into the ocean, where it came from.

This giving up is not a repenting.
It is a deep honoring of yourself.

When the ocean comes to you as a lover,
marry, at once, quickly for God's sake.

Don't postpone it. Existence has no better gift.
No amount of searching will find this.

A perfect falcon, for no reason,
has landed on your shoulder, and become yours.

*The Worm's Waking*

This is how a human being can change.
There is a worm
addicted to eating grape leaves.

Suddenly, he wakes up,
call it grace, whatever, something
wakes him, and he is no longer a worm.

He is the entire vineyard,
and the orchard too, the fruit, the trunks,
a growing wisdom and joy
that does not need to devour.

### *Talking through the Door (1)*

You said, Who's at the door?
        I said, Your slave.

You said, What do you want?
        To see you and bow.

We talked through the door. I claimed
a great love and that I had given up
what the world gives to be in that love.

You said, Such claims require a witness.
        I said, This longing, these tears.

You said, Discredited witnesses.
        I said, Surely not.

You said, Who did you come with?
        This majestic imagination you gave me.

Why did you come?
        The musk of your wine was in the air.

What is your intention?
        Friendship.

*Talking through the Door (2)*

Then you asked, Where have you been most comfortable?
      In the palace.

What did you see there?
      Amazing things.

Then why is it so desolate?
      Because all that can be taken away in a second.

Who can do that?
      This clear discernment.

Where can you live safely?
      In surrender.

Is there no threat of disaster?
      Only what comes in your street,
      inside your love.

Now silence. If I tell more of this conversation,
those listening would leave themselves.

There would be no door,
no roof or window either.

*Imagining Is Like*

Imagining is like feeling around
in a dark lane, or washing
your eyes with blood.

You *are* the truth
from foot to brow. Now,
what else would you like to know?

## Dark Sweetness

The ground turns green. A drum begins.
Commentaries on the heart arrive in seven volumes.

The pen puts its head down
to give a dark sweetness to the page.

Planets go wherever they want.
Venus sways near the North Star.
The moon holds on to Leo.

The host who has no self is here.
We look into each other's eyes.

A child is still a child
even after it has learned the alphabet.

Solomon lifts his morning cup to the mountains.
Sit down in this pavilion,
and don't listen to religious bickering.
Be silent as we absorb the spring.

### The Grasses

The same wind that uproots trees
makes the grasses shine.

The lordly wind loves the weakness
and the lowness of grasses.

The axe doesn't worry how thick the branches are.
It cuts them to pieces. But not the leaves.
It leaves the leaves alone.

The motion of the body, the inhaling-exhaling,
comes from the spirit, now angry, now peaceful.
Wind destroys, and wind protects.

*There is no reality but God,*
says the completely surrendered sheikh,
who is an ocean for all beings.
The levels of creation are straws in that ocean.

The movement of the straws comes from an agitation
in the water. When the ocean wants the straws calm,
it sends them close to shore. When it wants them
back in the deep surge, it does with them
as the wind does with the grasses.

# FEBRUARY 23

---

### *When I Am with You*

When I am with you, we stay up all night.
When you are not here, I can't go to sleep.

Praise God for these two insomnias.
And the difference between them.

### *Red Shirt*

Has anyone seen the boy who used to come here?
Round-faced troublemaker, quick to find a joke, slow
to be serious. Red shirt,
perfect coordination, sly,
strong muscles, with things always in his pocket.
Reed flute, ivory pick, polished
and ready for his talent.
You know that one.

Have you heard stories about him?
Pharaoh and the whole Egyptian world
collapsed for such a Joseph.
I would gladly spend years getting word
of him, even third- or fourth-hand.

*My Worst Habit*

My worst habit is I get so tired of winter
I become a torture to those I'm with.

If you are not here, nothing grows.
I lack clarity. My words
tangle and knot up.

How to cure bad water? Send it back to the river.
How to cure bad habits? Send me back to you.

When water gets caught in habitual whirlpools,
dig a way out through the bottom
to the ocean. There is a secret medicine
given only to those who hurt so hard
they can't hope.

The hopers would feel slighted if they knew.

Look as long as you can at the friend you love,
no matter whether that friend is moving away from you
or coming back toward you.

### Red

Red with shyness, the red
that became all the rosegarden reds.

The red distance,
red of the stove boiling water,
red of the mountain turning bloodred,
a mountain holding rubies secretly inside.

Do I love more you
or your modesty?

### *Body Intelligence (1)*

Your intelligence is always with you,
overseeing your body, even though
you may not be aware of its work.

If you start doing something
against your health, your intelligence
will eventually scold you.

If it had not been so lovingly close by,
and so constantly monitoring,
how could it rebuke?

You and your body's intelligence
are like the beauty and precision
of an astrolabe.

Together, you calculate how near
existence is to the sun.

Your intelligence is marvelously intimate.
It is not in front of you or behind,
or to the left or the right.

Now, my friend, try to describe how near
is the creator of your intelligence.

*Body Intelligence* (2)

There are guides
who can show you the way.
Use them.

But they will not satisfy your longing.
Keep wanting the connection with presence
with all your pulsing energy.

The throbbing vein
will take you further
than any thinking.

Muhammed said, Do not theorize
about essence. All speculations
are just more layers of covering.
Human beings love coverings.

They think the designs on the curtains
are what is being concealed.

Observe the wonders as they occur around you.
Do not claim them. Feel the artistry
moving through, and be silent.

# FEBRUARY 29

## *Dervishes*

You have heard of the ocean of nonexistence.
Try continually to give yourself to that ocean.

Every workshop has its foundations
set on that emptiness.

The master of all masters works with nothing.
The more such nothing comes into your work,
the more the presence will be there.

Dervishes gamble everything.
They lose and win the other,
the emptiness which animates this.

We have talked so much.
Remember what we have not said.

And keep working. Laziness and disdain
are not devotions. Your effort
will bring a result.

As dawn lightens, blow out the candle.
Dawn is in your eyes now.

# MARCH

## *I Have Five Things to Say*

I have five things to say,
five fingers to give into your grace.

First, when I was apart from you,
   this world did not exist, nor any other.
Second, whatever I was looking for was always you.
Third, why did I ever learn to count to three?
Fourth, my cornfield is burning!
Fifth, this finger stands for Rabia, and this
   is for someone else. Is there a difference?

Are these words or tears?
Is weeping speech? What shall I do, my love?
So he speaks, and everyone around
begins to cry with him, laughing crazily,
moaning in the spreading union of lover and beloved.

This is the true religion. All others
are thrown-away bandages beside it.
This is the *sema* of slavery and mastery
dancing together. This is not-being.

I know these dancers. Day and night
I sing their songs in this phenomenal cage.

### *There Is Some Kiss We Want*

There is some kiss we want
with our whole lives,
the touch of spirit on the body.

Seawater begs the pearl
to break its shell.

And the lily, how passionately
it needs some wild darling.

At night, I open the window
and ask the moon to come
and press its face against mine.
*Breathe into me.*

Close the language-door
and open the love-window.

The moon won't use the door,
only the window.

## *The Tent*

Outside, the freezing desert night.
This other night inside grows warm, kindling.
Let the landscape be covered with thorny crust.
We have a soft garden in here.
The continents blasted,
cities and little towns, everything
become a scorched, blackened ball.

The news we hear is full of grief for that future,
but the real news inside here
is there's no news at all.

## *This World Which Is Made of Our Love for Emptiness*

Praise to the emptiness that blanks out existence.
Existence: this place made from our love
for that emptiness!

Yet somehow comes emptiness,
this existence goes.
Praise to that happening over and over.

For years I pulled my own existence out of emptiness.
Then one swoop, one swing of the arm,
that work is over.
Free of who I was, free of presence, free
of dangerous fear, hope, free
of mountainous wanting.

The here-and-now mountain is a tiny piece
of a piece of straw
blown into emptiness.

These words I am saying so much begin to lose meaning.
Existence, emptiness, mountain, straw.
Words and what they try to say,
swept out the window, down the slant of the roof.

### *Strange Frenzy*

There is a strange frenzy in my head,
of birds flying,
each particle circulating on its own.
Is the one I love everywhere?

### The Milk of Millenia

I am part of the load
not rightly balanced.
I drop off in the grass
like the old cave-sleepers, to browse
wherever I fall.

For hundreds of thousands of years I have been dustgrains
floating and flying in the will of the air,
often forgetting ever being
in that state, but in sleep
I migrate back. I spring loose
from the four-branched, time-and-space cross,
this waiting room.

I walk out into a huge pasture.
I nurse the milk of millenia.

Everyone does this in different ways.
Knowing that conscious decisions
and personal memory
are much too small a place to live,
every human being streams at night
into the loving nowhere, or during the day,
in some absorbing work.

### A Tender Agony of Parting

A craftsman pulled a reed from the reedbed,
cut holes in it, and called it a human being.

Since then, it has been wailing
a tender agony of parting,
never mentioning the skill
that gave it life as a flute.

### *The Lame Goat*

You have seen a herd of goats
going down to the water.

The lame and dreamy goat
brings up the rear.

There are worried faces about that one,
but now they're laughing,

because look, as they return,
that one is leading.

There are many different ways of knowing.
The lame goat's kind is a branch
that traces back to the roots of presence.

Learn from the lame goat,
and lead the herd home.

### *The* You *Pronoun*

Someone asked once, What is love?

Be lost in me, I said. You will know love when that happens.

Love has no calculating in it. That is why it is said to be a quality of God and not of human beings. *God loves you* is the only possible sentence. The subject becomes the object so totally that it can't be turned around. Who will the *you* pronoun stand for if you say, *You love God?*

### *Buoyancy*

I saw you and became empty.
This emptiness, more beautiful than existence,
it obliterates existence, and yet when it comes,
existence thrives and creates more existence.

To praise is to praise
how one surrenders to the emptiness.

To praise the sun is to praise your own eyes.
Praise, the ocean. What we say, a little ship.

So the sea-journey goes on, and who knows where?
Just to be held by the ocean is the best luck
we could have. It is a total waking-up.

Why should we grieve that we have been sleeping?
It does not matter how long we've been unconscious.
We are groggy, but let the guilt go.

Feel the motions of tenderness
around you, the bouyancy.

## *Locked Out of Life*

Again it happens in my sleep.
A core of wakefulness opens.
But I have ways of ignoring that.

You say, How long will you beg from others,
when there are things born of you
that emperors want?

Why waste time in meanness?
Who else can say what you say to me?

If I could repeat it, people passing by
would be enlightened and go free.

You are an ocean in my chest
where everyone changes places,
believer-unbeliever, cynic-lover,
dervish-king.

Last night you came to my sleep
asking, How are you?

Locked out of life, waiting, weeping.

*Sufi Masters (1)*

Sufi masters are those
whose spirits existed before the world.
Before the body, they lived many lifetimes.
Before seeds went into the ground, they harvested wheat.
Before there was an ocean, they strung pearls.
While the great meeting was going on about bringing
human beings into existence, they stood up to their chins
in wisdom water. When some of the angels opposed creation,
the Sufi sheikhs laughed and clapped among themselves.

Before materiality, they knew what it was like
to be trapped inside matter. Before there was a night sky,
they saw Saturn. Before wheat grains, they tasted bread.
With no mind, they thought. Immediate intuition to them
is the simplest act of consciousness, what to others
would be epiphany. Much of our thought is of the past,
or the future. They are free of those.

Before a mine is dug, they judge coins.
Before vineyards, they know the excitements to come.
In July, they feel December. In unbroken sunlight,
they find shade. In *fana*, the state where all objects
dissolve, they recognize objects.

### *Sufi Masters* (2)

The open sky drinks from their circling cup.
The sun wears the gold of their generosity.
When two of them meet, they are no longer two.
They are one, and six hundred thousand.
The ocean waves are their closest likeness
when wind makes from unity the numerous.

This happened to the sun, and it broke into rays.
The disc of the sun does exist, but if you see
only the ray-bodies, you may have doubts.
The human-divine combination is a oneness.
Plurality, the apparent separation into rays.

Friends, we are traveling together.
Throw off your tiredness. Let me show you
one tiny spot of the beauty that cannot be spoken.
I am like an ant that has gotten into the granary,
ludicrously happy, and trying to lug out
a grain that is way too big.

---

### *Flood Residue*

The taste of today is not that of yesterday.
A pot boils over.

A watchman calls down the ladder,
Did you hear the commotion last night
from the seventh level?

Saturn turns to Venus and tells her
to play the strings more gently.
Taurus milk runs red. Leo slinks from the sky.

Strange signs, because of a word
that comes from the soul
to help us escape from speaking and concepts.

I answer the nightwatchman,
You will have to assign meanings
for these ominous events.

I have been set free from the hunt,
the catching and the being caught,
to rest in these dregs
of flood residue, pure and empty.

### A Poem in a Letter

Before death takes away what you are given,
give away what is there to give.

No dead person grieves for his death. He mourns only what
he didn't do. Why did I wait? Why did I not . . . ? Why did I
neglect to . . . ?

I cannot think of better advice to send. I hope you like it.
May you stay in your infinity.

Peace.

*One hundred and forty-seven of Rumi's letters
survive. Many of them contain lines of poetry composed
while writing the letters.*

### *Humble Living*

Humble living does not diminish. It fills.
Going back to a simpler self gives wisdom.

When a man makes up a story for his child,
he becomes a father and a child
together, listening.

### Morning Water and a Poet

We learn this from a drunken king
who wakes up hungover and sick,
asking for two things, a morning drink of water,
and *Let it be brought by a poet.*

There is a tradition that the wine
of nonexistence makes us God-drunk.
Intoxicated that way, we are purified.

There is a kind of poet
whose poetry pours that wine,

and there is another poet who makes us want
the red wine and the white.
The two poets may even have the same name.

Look inside form. Read with your soul
this *Masnavi.* Let it bring you
morning water and a poet.

*Wax*

When I see you and how you are,
I close my eyes to the other.
For your Solomon's seal I become wax
throughout my body. I wait to be light.
I give up opinions on all matters.
I become the reed flute for your breath.

You were inside my hand.
I kept reaching around for something.
I was inside your hand, but I kept asking questions
of those who know very little.

I must have been incredibly simple or drunk or insane
to sneak into my own house and steal money,
to climb over my own fence and take my own vegetables.
But no more. I have gotten free of that ignorant fist
that was pinching and twisting my secret self.

The universe and the light of the stars come through me.
I am the crescent moon put up
over the gate to the festival.

### *Dissolver of Sugar*

Dissolver of sugar, dissolve me,
if this is the time.
Do it gently with a touch of a hand, or a look.
Every morning I wait at dawn. That's when
it has happened before. Or do it suddenly
like an execution. How else
can I get ready for death?

You breathe without a body, like a spark.
You grieve, and I begin to feel lighter.
You keep me away with your arm,
but the keeping away is pulling me in.

### The Waterwheel

Stay together, friends.
Don't scatter and sleep.

Our friendship is made
of being awake.

The waterwheel accepts water
and turns and gives it away,
weeping.

That way it stays in the garden,
whereas another roundness
rolls through a dry riverbed looking
for what it thinks it wants.

Stay here, quivering with each moment
like a drop of mercury.

### *Spring Is Christ*

Everyone has eaten and fallen asleep.
The house is empty.

We walk out to the garden to let the apple
meet the peach, to carry messages
between rose and jasmine.

Spring is Christ,
raising martyred plants from their shrouds.

A leaf trembles. I tremble
in the wind-beauty like silk from Turkestan.
The censer fans into flame.

This wind is the Holy Spirit.
The trees are Mary.
Watch how husband and wife play subtle games
with their hands. Strings of cloudy pearls
are thrown across the lovers,
as is the marriage custom.

We talk about this and that. There is no rest
except on these branching moments.

*Quietness*

Inside this new love, die.
Your way begins on the other side.
Become the sky.
Take an axe to the prison wall.
Escape.
Walk out like someone suddenly born into color.
Do it now.
You are covered with thick cloud.
Slide out the side. Die,
and be quiet. Quietness is the surest sign
that you have died.
Your old life was a frantic running
from silence.

The speechless full moon
comes out now.

## MARCH 23

### *The Sun Is Love*

The sun is love. The lover,
a speck circling the sun.

A spring wind moves to dance
any branch that isn't dead.

*Spring*

Again the violet bows to the lily.
Again, the rose is tearing off her gown.

The green ones have come from the other world,
tipsy like the breeze up to some new foolishness.

Again, near the top of the mountain
the anemone's sweet features appear.

The hyacinth speaks formally to the jasmine.
Peace be with you. And peace to you, lad.
Come walk with me in the meadow.

The Friend is here like water in the stream,
like a lotus on the water.

The ringdove comes asking, *Where*,
*where* is the Friend? With one note
the nightingale indicates the rose.

Many things must be left unsaid because it is late,
but whatever conversation we have not had
tonight, we will have tomorrow.

---

### *A Bowl*

Imagine the time the particle you are
returns where it came from.

The family darling comes home. Wine,
without being contained in cups,
is handed around.

A red glint appears in a granite outcrop,
and suddenly the whole cliff turns to ruby.

At dawn I walked along with a monk
on his way to the monastery.

We do the same work, I told him.
We suffer the same.

He gave me a bowl, and I saw.
The soul has *this* shape.

Shams, and actual sunlight, help me now,
being in the middle of being
partly in myself, and partly outside.

### *The Orchard*

Come to the orchard in spring.
There is light and wine and sweethearts
in the pomegranate flowers.

If you do not come, these do not matter.
If you do come, these do not matter.

---

### *A Wished-For Song*

You are song, a wished-for song.
Go through the ear to the center,
where sky is, where wind,
where silent knowing.

Put seeds and cover them.
Blades will sprout
where you do your work.

## *Joseph*

Joseph has come, the handsome one of this age,
a victory banner floating over spring flowers.

Those of you whose work it is to wake the dead,
get up. This is a work day.

The lion that hunts lions charges into the meadow.
Yesterday and the day before are gone.
The beautiful coin of now slaps down in your hand.

Start the drumbeat. Everything we have said
about the Friend is true. The beauty of that
peacefulness makes the whole world restless.

Spread your love-robe out to catch
what sifts down from the ninth level.

You heart closed up in a chest, open,
for the Friend is entering you.

You feet, it is time to dance.
Don't talk about the old man.

He is young again. And don't mention
the past. Do you understand?
The beloved is here.

*How We Move Inside Grace* (1)

When our water here
becomes saturated with pollution,
it gets led back to the original water, the ocean.

After a year of receiving starlight,
the water returns, sweeping new robes along.

Where have you been? In the ocean of purity.
Now I am ready for more cleaning work.
If there were no impurity, what would water do?
It shows its glory in how it washes a face,
and in other qualities as well,
the way it grows the grass
and lifts a ship across to another port.

When the river slows with the weight of silt
and corruption, it grows sad and prays,
Lord, what you gave me I gave others.
Is there more? Can you give more?

Clouds draw the water up to become rain;
the ocean takes the river back into itself.

What this means is
we often need to be refreshed.

### *How We Move Inside Grace* (2)

Water is the story of how we are helped.
Hot baths prepare us to enter the fire.
Only salamanders can go directly in
without an intermediary, salamanders and Abraham.

The rest of us need guidance from water.
Satisfaction comes from God,
but to get there you need to eat bread.

Beauty comes from the presence,
but those of us in bodies
must walk in a garden to feel it.

When this body-medium goes, we will see directly
the light that lives in the chest.

The qualities of water are showing us
how we move inside grace.

### *A Turning Night*

This moment, this love, comes to rest in me,
many beings in one being.

In one wheatgrain a thousand sheaf-stacks.
Inside the needle's eye, a turning night of stars.

# APRIL

## The Diver's Clothes

You are sitting here with us,
but you are also out walking in a field at dawn.

You are yourself the animal we hunt
when you come with us on the hunt.

You are in your body
like a plant is solid in the ground,
yet you are wind.

You are the diver's clothes
lying empty on the beach.
You are the fish.

In the ocean are many bright strands
and many dark strands like veins that are seen
when a wing is lifted up.

Your hidden self is blood in those,
those veins that are lute strings
that make ocean music,
not the sad edge of surf,
but the sound of no shore.

*Our Closeness*

Friend, our closeness is this.
Anywhere you put your foot
feel me in the firmness under you.

How is it with this love,
I see your world and not you?

### *On Resurrection Day*

On Resurrection Day your body testifies against you.
Your hand says, I stole money.
Your lips, I said meanness.
Your feet, I went where I shouldn't.
Your genitals, me too.

They will make your praying sound hypocritical.
Let the body's doings speak openly now,
without your saying a word,

as a student's walking behind a teacher
says, This one knows more clearly
than I the way.

### *Already Under*

Late by myself, in the boat of myself,
no light and no land anywhere,
cloudcover thick.

I try to stay just above the surface,
yet I am already under
and living within the ocean.

### Urgency

When the captain sees the girl,
he immediately falls in love with her
like the Caliph.

Don't laugh at this.
His loving is also part of infinite love,
without which the world does not evolve.

Forms move from inorganic to vegetation
to selves endowed with spirit
through the urgency of every love
that wants to come to perfection.

---

### *Blessing*

I want to be where
your bare foot walks,

because maybe before you step,
you will look at the ground.
I want that blessing.

## *This Day*

This is not a day for asking questions,
not a day on any calendar.

This day is conscious of itself.
This day is a lover, bread and gentleness.

### Childsplay

There is no one with intelligence
in our town except that man over there
playing with the children.

He has keen, fiery insight
and vast dignity like the nightsky,
but he conceals it in childsplay.

### *Let Yourself Be Drawn*

You miss the garden,
because you want a small fig from a random tree.
You do not meet the beautiful woman.
You are joking with an old crone.
It makes me cry how she detains you,
stinking-mouthed with a hundred talons,
putting her head over the roof edge to call down,
tasteless fig, fold over fold, empty
as a dry-rotten garlic.

She has you tight by the belt,
even though there is no flower
and no milk inside her body.

Death will open your eyes
to what her face is: leather spine
of a black lizard. No more advice.

Let yourself be silently drawn
by the stronger pull of what you really love.

## Burnt Kabob

Last year I admired wines.
This year I am wandering inside the red world.
Last year I gazed at the fire.
This year I am burnt kabob.

Thirst drove me down to the water,
where I drank the moon's reflection.
Now I am a lion staring up
totally lost in love with the thing itself.

Do not ask questions about longing.
Look in my face.

Soul-drunk, body-ruined, these two
sit helpless in a wrecked wagon.
Neither knows how to fix it.
And my heart, I would say it is more
like a donkey sunk in a mudhole,
struggling and miring deeper.

But listen to me. For one moment
quit being sad. Hear blessings
dropping their blossoms
around you. God.

### Be Your Note

Remember the lips where wind-breath
originated, and let your note be clear.

Don't try to end it.
*Be* your note.

I'll show you how it's enough.
Go up on the roof at night
in this city of the soul.

Let everyone climb on their roofs
and sing their notes.

Sing loud!

## *An Egypt That Does Not Exist*

I want to say words that flame
as I say them, but I keep quiet
and don't try to make both worlds
fit in one mouthful.

I keep secret in myself
an Egypt that does not exist.
Is that good or bad? I don't know.

For years I gave away sexual love
with my eyes. Now I don't.

I am not in any one place.
I do not have a name for what I give away.

Whatever Shams gave,
that you can have from me.

---

### *An Evolving Course*

We began as a mineral.
We emerged into plant life and into
the animal state, and then to being human.

And always we have forgotten our former states,
except in early spring,
when we dimly recall being green again.

That is how a young person turns
toward a teacher, how a baby leans
toward the breast, without knowing
the secret of its desire,
yet turning instinctively.

So humankind is being led along
an evolving course through this migration
of intelligences, and though we seem
to be sleeping, there is an inner wakefulness
that directs the dream.

It will eventually startle us back
to the truth of who we are.

## *Fog*

As fog rising off the sea
covers the sea,

so it is noble work to build
coherent philosophical discourses,

but they block the sun of truth.
See God's qualities as an ocean

and this world as foam
on the purity of that ocean.

Here is the mystery.
This intricate, astonishing world
is proof of God's existence,
even as it covers the beauty.

One flake from the wall of a goldmine
does not give much idea
what it is like

when the sun shines in
and turns the air
and the workers golden.

## *Bewilderment*

There are many guises for intelligence.
One part of you is gliding in a high windstream,
while your more ordinary notions
take little steps and peck at the ground.

Conventional knowledge is death to our souls,
and it is not really ours. It is laid on.
Yet we keep saying we find "rest" in these "beliefs."

We must become ignorant of what we have been taught
and be instead bewildered.

Run from what is profitable and comfortable.
Distrust anyone who praises you.
Give your investment money, and the interest
on the capital, to those who are actually destitute.

Forget safety. Live where you fear to live.
Destroy your reputation. Be notorious.
I have tried prudent planning long enough.
From now on, I'll be mad.

### The Buddhist Sufi

Last night my soul asked a question of existence.
Why are you upsidedown with flames in your belly?
Happy, unhappy, indigo-orange like the sky?

Why are you an off-balance wobbling millstone,
like the Buddhist Sufi, Ibrahim Balkhi,
who was king, beggar, buddha, and dervish?

Existence answers, All this was made
by the one who hides inside you.

You are like a beautiful new bride,
quick to anger, stubborn,
hot, naked, but still veiled.

### Half-Heartedness

Gamble everything for love,
if you are a true human being.
If not, leave this gathering.

Half-heartedness does not reach
into majesty. You set out
to find God, but then you keep
stopping for long periods
at mean-spirited roadhouses.

## A Small Green Island

There is a small green island
where one white cow lives alone, a meadow of an island.

The cow grazes till nightfull, full and fat,
but during the night she panics
and grows thin as a single hair.
What shall I eat tomorrow? There is nothing left.
By dawn the grass has grown up again, waist-high.
The cow starts eating and by dark
the meadow is clipped short.

She is full of strength and energy, but she panics
in the dark as before and grows abnormally thin overnight.
The cow does this over and over,
and this is all she does.

She never thinks, This meadow has never failed
to grow back. Why should I be afraid every night
that it won't. The cow is the bodily soul.
The island field is this world where that grows
lean with fear and fat with blessing, lean and fat.

White cow, don't make yourself miserable
with what's to come, or not to come.

### *Sheba's Throne (1)*

When the Queen of Sheba came to Solomon,
she left behind her kingdom and her wealth,
the same way lovers leave their reputations.

Her servants meant nothing to her,
less than a rotten onion.
Her palaces and orchards, so many piles of dung.

She heard the inner meaning of LA: *No.*
She came to Solomon with nothing, except her throne.

As the writer's pen becomes a friend,
as the tool the workman uses day after day
becomes deeply familiar, so her filigreed throne
was her one attachment.

It was a large throne and difficult to transport,
because it could not be taken apart,
being as cunningly put together as the human body.

## *Sheba's Throne* (2)

Solomon saw that her heart was open to him
and that the throne would soon be left behind.

Let her bring it, he said.
It will soon become a lesson to her.
She can look at that throne
and see how far she has come.

In the same way God keeps the process
of generation constantly before us.
The smooth skin and the semen,
the wet of desire and the growing embryo.

When you see a pearl on the bottom,
you reach through the foam and the broken sticks
on the surface. When the sun comes up,
you forget about the problem of locating
the constellation of Scorpio.

Inside the splendor of union,
the attractions of duality seem poignant
and lovely, but much less interesting.

---

## *I, You, He, She, We*

I, you, he, she, we.
In the garden of mystic lovers
these are not true distinctions.

### *Your Features*

The light you give off
did not come from a pelvis.

Your features did not begin in semen.
Do not try to hide inside anger
radiance that cannot be hidden.

*How You Are with Me*

God spoke to Moses,
You are the one I have chosen,
and I love you.

Moses replies, I feel the generosity,
but say what it is in me
that causes your love.

God explains, You have seen
a little child with its mother.
It does not know anyone else exists.

The mother praises or scolds,
a little slap perhaps,
but still the child reaches
to be held by her.

Disappointment, elation,
there is only one direction
that the child turns.

That is how
you are with me.

*Night Prayer*

Now I lay me down
to stay awake.

Pray the Lord my soul to take
into your wakefulness,

so that I can get this one bit
of wisdom clear.

Grace comes to forgive
and then forgive again.

### *The Way That Moves as You Move*

Some commentary on the quatrain:
*As you start on the way, the way appears.*
*When you cease to be, real being comes.*

This is how you slip through
to your non-spatial home.

Think of how you came into this world.
Can you explain how that was? No? The same way
that you came is the way you will leave.

You wander landscapes in your dreams.
How did you get there? Close your eyes and surrender,
and find yourself in the city of God.

But you are still looking for admiration.
You love how your customers look at you.
You love to sit at the head of the assembly.
You close your eyes and see people applauding
as surely as an owl shuts and sees the forest.

You live in an admiration-world,
but what do you offer your admirers?
If you had true spirit-gifts to give,
you would not think of customers.

## *The Well*

We seem to be sitting still,
but we are actually moving,
and the fantasies of phenomena
are sliding though us,
like ideas through curtains.

They go to the well of deep love
inside each of us.

They fill their jars there
and they leave.

There is a source they come from,
and a fountain inside here.

Be generous and grateful.
Confess when you're not.

We cannot know
what the divine intelligence has in mind.

Who am I,
standing in the midst of this
thought-traffic?

### *The Sight of a Soul*

One of the marvels of the world
is the sight of a soul sitting in prison
with the key in its hand.

Covered with dust,
with a cleansing waterfall an inch away.

A young man rolls from side to side,
though the bed is comfortable
and a pillow holds his head.

He has a living master, yet he wants more,
and there is more.

If a prisoner had not lived outside,
he would not detest the dungeon.

Desiring knows there is a satisfaction
beyond this. Straying maps the path.

A secret freedom opens
through a crevice you can barely see.

The awareness a wine drinker wants
cannot be tasted in wine, but that failure
brings his deep thirst closer.

## The Question (1)

One dervish to another, What was your vision
of God's presence? I haven't seen anything,
but for the sake of conversation, I will tell you a story.

The presence is there in front of me.
A fire on the left, a lovely stream on the right.
One group walks toward the fire, *into* the fire.
Another toward the sweet flowing water.
No one knows which are blessed and which not.
Whoever walks into the fire appears suddenly
in the stream. A head goes underwater
and that head pokes out of the fire.

Most people guard against going into the fire
and so end up in it. Those who love the water
of pleasure and make it their devotion
are cheated with this reversal. The trickery goes further.
The voice of the fire tells the truth, saying
*I am not fire. I am fountainhead.*
*Come into me and don't mind the sparks.*

If you are a friend of the presence,
fire is your water.

### *The Question (2)*

You should wish to have a hundred thousand sets
of mothwings, so you could burn them away, one set a night.

The moth sees light and goes into fire. You should see fire
and go to the light. Fire is what of God is world-consuming.
Water, world-protecting.

Somehow each gives the appearance of the other.
To these eyes you have now, what looks like water burns.
What looks like fire is a great relief to be inside.

You have seen a magician make a bowl of rice
seem a dish of tiny, live worms. Before an assembly, with one
    breath he made the floor swarm with scorpions
that were not there. How much more amazing God's tricks.
    Generation after generation lies down defeated, they think,
but they are like a woman underneath a man, circling him.

One molecule-mote-second of considering
this reversal of comfort and pain
is better than any attending ritual.

That splinter of intelligence is substance.
The fire and water themselves?
Accidental, done with mirrors.

## When Living Itself

If the beloved is everywhere,
the lover is a veil,

but when living itself becomes
the Friend, lovers disappear.

# MAY

### *The Way You Make Love*

The way you make love
is the way God will be with you.


*This is Rumi's variation on the golden rule.*

### *Response to Your Question*

Why ask about behavior
when you are soul-essence
and a way of seeing into presence?
Plus you are with us. How could you worry?

You may as well free a few words
from your vocabulary: *why* and *how* and *impossible*.
Open the mouth-cage and let those fly away.

We were all born by accident,
but still this wandering caravan
will make camp in perfection.

Forget the nonsense categories
of *there* and *here*.
Race and nation and religion.
Starting-point and destination.

You are soul and you are love,
not a sprite or an angel or a human being.
You are a Godman-womanGod-manGod-Godwoman.

No more questions now
as to what it is we are doing here.

---

### *What Was Said to the Rose*

What was said to the rose that made it open
was said to me here in my chest.

What was told the cypress
that made it strong and straight,
what was whispered the jasmine
so it is what it is,
whatever made sugarcane sweet,
whatever was said to the inhabitants
of the town of Chigil in Turkestan
that makes them so handsome,
whatever lets the pomegranate flower
blush like a human face,
that is being said to me now. I blush.

Whatever put eloquence in language,
that's happening here.

The great warehouse doors open,
and I fill with gratitude,
chewing a piece of sugarcane,
in love with the one
to whom every *that* belongs.

## *The Most Alive Moment*

The most alive moment comes
when those who love each other
meet each other's eyes
and in what flows between them then.

To see your face in a crowd of others,
or alone on a frightening street,
I weep for that.

Our tears improve the earth.
The time you scolded me,
your gratitude, your laughing,
always your qualities increase the soul.

Seeing you is a wine
that does not muddle or numb.

We sit inside the cypress shadow
where amazement and clear thought
twine their slow growth into us.

*Cry Out*

Crying out loud and weeping are great resources.
A nursing mother, all she does
is wait to hear her child.

Just a little beginning-whimper
and she's there.

Cry out. Do not be stolid and silent
with your pain. Lament,
and let the milk of loving flow into you.

The hard rain and the wind
are ways the cloud has
to take care of us.

## The Old Poet's Waking

The old man's heart woke,
no longer in love with treble and bass,
without weeping or laughter.

In the true bewilderment of soul
he went out beyond any seeking, beyond words
and telling, drowned in the beauty,
drowned beyond deliverance.

Waves cover the old man.

Nothing more can be said of him.

He has shaken out his robe,
and there's nothing in it anymore.

There is a chase where a falcon
dives into the forest
and does not come back up.

Every moment, the sunlight
is totally empty and totally full.

*Daring Enough to Finish*

Face that lights my face,
you spin intelligence into these particles
I am. Your wind shivers my tree.

You make my dance daring enough to finish.
No more timidity. Let fruit fall,
and wind turn my roots up in the air,
done with patient waiting.

*The Vigil*

Lovers cannot sleep
when they feel the privacy
of the beloved all around them.

Someone who is thirsty
may sleep for a little while,
but he or she will dream of water,
a full jar beside a creek,
or the spirit-water you get
from another person.

All night, listen to the conversation.
Stay up. This moment is all there is.

## *The Wandering Kings*

The King of Tabuk went on like this,
praising Imra'u 'l-Qays, and talking theology
and philosophy. Imra'u 'l-Qays kept silent.
Then suddenly he leaned and whispered something
in the second king's ear, and that second
that second king became a wanderer too.
They walked out of town hand in hand.
No royal belts, no thrones.
This is what love does and continues to do.

It tastes like honey to adults and milk to children.
Love is the last thirty-pound bale.
When you load it on, the boat tips over.

So they wandered around China like birds pecking
at bits of grain. They rarely spoke because
of the dangerous seriousness of the secret they knew.

That love-secret spoken pleasantly, or in irritation,
severs a hundred thousand heads in one swing.

A love-lion grazes in the soul's pasture,
while the scimitar of this secret approaches.
It is a killing better than any living.
All that world-power wants, really, is this weakness.

## *Whatever You Really See*

A human being is essentially
a spirit-eye.

Whatever you really see,
you *are* that.

### Constant Conversation

Who is luckiest in this whole orchestra? The reed.
Its mouth touches your lips to learn music.
All reeds, sugarcane especially, think only
of this chance. They sway in the canebrake,
free in the many ways they dance.

Without you the instruments would die.
One sits close beside you. Another takes a long kiss.
The tambourine begs, *Touch my skin, so I can be myself.*
Let me feel you enter each limb bone by bone,
that what died last night can be whole today.

Why live some soberer way and feel you ebbing out?
I won't do it.
Either give me enough wine or leave me alone,
now that I know how it is
to be with you in a constant conversation.

### *Presences*

Listen to presences inside poems.
Let them take you where they will.

Follow those private hints,
and never leave the premises.

*The Truest Devotion*

Moses ran after the shepherd.
He followed the bewildered footprints,
in one place moving straight like a castle
across a chessboard.
        Then sideways, like a bishop.
Now surging, like a wave cresting.
          Now sliding down
like a fish, with always his feet
        making geomancy
symbols in the sand,
      recording his wandering state.

Moses finally caught up with him.
I was wrong. God has revealed to me
that there are no rules for worship.

Say whatever and however your loving tells you to.
Your sweet blasphemy is the truest devotion.
Through you a whole world is freed.

Loosen your tongue
and don't worry what comes out.
It is all the light of the spirit.

## MAY 14

*Music Master*

You that love lovers,
this is your home. Welcome.

In the midst of making form,
love made this form that melts form,
with love for the door
and soul for the vestibule.

Watch the dust grains
moving in the light near the window.

Their dance is our dance.

We rarely hear the inward music,
but we are all dancing to it nevertheless,
directed by the one who teaches us,
the pure joy of the sun,
our music master.

### The Uses of Fear

A donkey turning a millstone is not trying
to press oil from sesame seed. He is fleeing the blow
that was just struck and hoping to avoid the next.

For the same reason, the ox takes a load
of baggage wherever you want him to.
Shopkeepers work for themselves,
not for the flow of communal exchange.

We look to ease our pain, and this keeps civilization
moving along. Fear is the architect here.
Fear keeps us working near the ark.

Some human beings are safe havens.
Be companions with them. Others may seem to be friends,
but they are really consuming your essence
like donkeys lapping sherbet. Detach from them,
and feel your flexibility returning.
The inner moisture that lets you bend
into a basket handle is a quickening inside
that no one is ever afraid of.

Sometimes though, it is fear, a contracting,
that brings you into the presence.

### *The Lord of Beauty*

The lord of beauty enters the soul
as a man walks into an orchard in spring.

Come into me that way again.
Like a fresh idea in an artist's mind,
you fashion things before they come into being.

You sweep the floor like the man
who keeps the doorway.

When you brush a form clean,
it becomes what it truly is.

You guard your silence perfectly
like a waterbag that does not leak.

You live where Shams lives,
because your heart-donkey
was strong enough to take you there.

### *The Pickaxe* (1)

Some commentary on *I was a hidden treasure,*
*and I desired to be known.*

Tear down this house.
A hundred thousand new houses can be built
from the transparent yellow carnelian
buried beneath it, and the only way to get to that
is to do the work of demolition,
and then the digging beneath the foundation.

With that value in hand all the new construction
will be done without effort. And anyway, sooner or later,
the house will fall on its own.

The jewel treasure will be uncovered,
but it will not be yours then.
The buried wealth is your pay
for doing the demolition,
the pick and shovel work.

If you wait and just let it happen,
you will bite your hand and say,
I did not do as I knew I should have.

### *The Pickaxe* (2)

This is a rented house.
You do not own the deed.

You have a lease, and you have set up
a little shop where you barely make a living
sewing patches on torn clothing.

Yet only a few feet underneath
are two veins, pure red and bright gold carnelian.

Quick. Take the pickaxe and pry the foundation.
You have got to quit this seamstress work.

What does the patch-sewing mean, you ask.
Eating and drinking. The heavy cloak
of the body is always getting torn.

You patch it with food
and other restless ego-satisfactions.

Rip up one board from the floor
and look into the basement.
You may see two glints in the dirt.

*My First Love Story*

The minute I heard my first love story
I started looking for you,
not knowing how blind that was.

Lovers don't finally meet somewhere.
They are in each other all along.

### Some Song or Something

Birdsong brings relief
to my longing.

I am just as ecstatic as they are,
but with nothing to say.

Please, universal soul, practice
some song, or something, through me.

*The Nightingale's Way*

A bird delegation comes to Solomon
complaining, Why is it
you never criticise the nightingale?

Because my way, the nightingale explains
for Solomon, is different.
Mid-March to mid-June I sing.

The other nine months,
while you continue chirping,
I am silent.

---

### *Having Nothing*

Whatever comes, comes from a need,
a sore distress, a hurting want.

Mary's pain made the baby Jesus.
Her womb opened its lips
and spoke the Word.

Every part of you has a secret language.
Your hands and your feet say what you have done.

Every need brings in what's needed.
Pain bears its cure like a child.

Having nothing produces provisions.
Ask a difficult question,
and the marvelous answer appears.

Build a ship, and there will be water
to float it. The tender-throated infant cries,
and milk drips from the mother's breast.

Be thirsty for the ultimate water.
Then be ready for what will come
pouring from the spring.

### *These Lights*

Inside water, a waterwheel turns.
A star circulates with the moon.

We live in the night ocean wondering,
*What are these lights?*

## *Flowers Open*

Flowers open every night
across the sky, a breathing peace,
and sudden flame catching.

## MAY 25

### I Met One Traveling

In the evening between sleep and waking
I met one traveling. He was the light of consciousness.
His body was soul, his pure wisdom apparent
in his beautiful face.

He praises me for a while, then scolds.
You sit on the seven-sky throne, in prison.
The sign of Gemini has set a table for you,
yet you stick your head down a drainhole again.

Essence is not nourished with food and sleep.
Do no one any harm in this timefield
of short crops where what you sow comes up very quickly.
You try to accomplish things, to win,
to reach goals. This is not the true situation.
Put the whole world in ambition's stomach,
it will never be enough.

Assume you get everything you want.
Assume you have it now. What's the point?
The next moment you die.

Friend, the youth you have lived is ending.
You sleep a drunken dreamless sleep
with no sense what morning you could wake inside.

### *Discipline*

Don't avoid discipline.
You have learned ways to make a living
for your body. Now learn to support
your soul. You wear fine clothing.
How do you dress your spirit?

This world is a playground
where children pretend to have shops.

Sometimes when they wrestle,
it may look like sex,
but none of it is real.

They exchange imaginary money.
Night comes, and they go home tired
with nothing in their hands.

*Certain Sunfish*

If you put on shoes that are too tight and walk out
across an empty plain, you will not feel the freedom
of the place unless you take off your shoes.
Your shoe-constriction has you confined.
At night before sleeping you take off the tight shoes,
and your soul releases into a place it knows.
Dream and glide deeper.

Physical existence is so cramped. We grow old and bentover
like embryos. Nine months passes; it is time to be born.
The lamb wants to graze green daylight.
There are ways of being born twice, of coming
to where you fly, not individually like birds,
but as the sun moves with its bride, sincerity.

Loaves of bread remind us of sunlight,
but when we are inside that orb, we lose interest
in building ovens, in millwork and the preparation
of fields before the planting.

Fish love the ocean. Snakes move like earth-fish
inside a mountain, well away from seawater.
Certain sunfish, though, turn snakes
into ocean-lovers.

## A Grape

If you would say I don't exist,
I would be grateful.

When **this** longing makes me disreputable,
then I have a little self-respect.

A vine begins to become wine
when you say, *Pressure is necessary
to burst open.*

### *The Healing Presence*

I go to the one who can cure me and say,
I have a hundred things wrong. Can you combine them
   to one?

I thought you were dead. I was, but I caught your fragrance
again, and came back to life.

Gently, his hand on my chest.
Which tribe are you from? This tribe.

He begins to treat my illness.
If I am angry and aggressive, he gives me wine.
I quit fighting. I take off my clothes.
I lie down. I sing in the circle of singers.
I roar and break cups, even big jars.
Some people worship golden calves.
I am the mangy calf who worships love.

The healing presence has called me from the hole I hid in.
My soul, if I am agile or stumbling, confused
or in my true being, it is all you.

Sometimes the sleek arrow.
Other times a worn leather thumbguard.
You bring me where everything circles.
Now you put the lid back on the wine vat, pure quiet.

### *Your First Eyes*

A lover has four streams inside,
of water, wine, honey, and milk.

Find those in yourself and pay no attention
to what so-and-so says about such-and-such.

The rose does not care
if someone calls it a thorn, or a jasmine.

Ordinary eyes categorize human beings.
That one is a Zoroastrian. This one a Muslim.

Walk instead with the other vision given you,
your first eyes. Bow to the essence
in a human being. Do not be content
with judging people good and bad.
Grow out of that.

The great blessing is that Shams
has poured a strength into the ground
that lets us wait and trust the waiting.

*The Nothing of Roselight*

Death comes, and what we thought
we needed loses importance.

The living shiver, focused
on a muscular dark hand,
rather than the glowing cup it holds
or the toast being proposed.

In that same way love enters
your life, and the I, the ego,
a corrupt, self-absorbed king,
dies during the night.

Let him go.
Breathe cold new air,
the nothing of roselight.

# JUNE

### The Flower's Eye

Find me near the flower's eye
that takes in provocation
and begins to grow.

Love is a baby that struggles
and fights, stops nursing, then runs out
through the door, escaping as a fire
jumping to the next burn.

---

### Inside a Country Dialect

A human being is like the rod
Moses held or the words
that Jesus said.

The outer is just a piece of wood,
or mouth-sounds of a country dialect,
whose inner parts can divide
the green ocean and make the dead
sit up and smile.

You see the far-off tents
of an encampment. You go closer.

There is a dust-shape, someone walking near.
Inside that, a man, bright eyes
and the strength of his presence.

When Moses returns from the wilderness
where he has gone alone,
Mount Sinai begins to dance.

## A Great Wagon

When I see your face, the stones start spinning.
You appear. All studying wanders.
I lose my place.

Water turns pearly.
Fire dies down and does not consume.

In your presence I do not want
what I thought I wanted,
those three little hanging lamps.

Inside your face the ancient manuscripts
seem like rusty mirrors.
You breathe, and new shapes appear.

The music of a desire as widespread as spring
begins to move like a great wagon.

Drive slowly.
Some of us walking alongside are lame.

### As a Wick Does

There is nourishment like bread
that feeds one part of your life,
nourishment like light for another.

There are many rules about restraint
with the former, but only one rule
for the latter, *Never be satisfied.*

Eat and drink the soul substance
as a wick does with the oil it soaks in.
Give light to the company.

### *Up to the Neck*

I sat long enough in fire.
Now I am up to my neck
in the water of union.

You say, Up to the neck
is not enough.

Make your head your foot
and descend into love.
There is no up-to-the-neck union.

I say, But for the sake of your garden
I sat up to my neck in blood.

You say, Yes, you escaped
the alluring world, but not yourself.

You are the magician
caught in his own trickery.

Cut the breath of self and be silent.
Language cannot come from your throat
as you choke and go under.

*No Need to Ask*

The one who brings wine pours again,
no need to ask.

Do you ask the moon to rise
and give its light?

When ranks of soldiers dissolve,
dismissed for a holiday,

when a lost hand reaches
to touch the rescuing hand,

when a candle next to a mirrored
sconce gets lit,

your presence enters my soul.

### Again

Again, the sharp new moon blade.
Again we walk a garden
with the lily's clever talking around us.

Green satin no tailor sews,
trees putting on their hats.

A drumming begins, and we play along
on the drums of our stomachs.

The lake that was ice and iron
now is ridged in the wind like David's chainmail.

A voice says to the herbs, Rise up.
The mystic crane returns.
The humiliated ones dress and show
their heads in windows again.

There is a public concert on the tomb of January.
The willow shakes its head.

Those we thought were lost are back.
How the sun is with plants
is evidence enough.

*Father Reason*

The universe is a form of divine law,
your reasonable father.

When you feel ungrateful to him,
the shapes of the world seem mean and ugly.

Make peace with that father, the elegant patterning,
and every experience will fill with immediacy.

Because I love this, I am never bored.
Beauty constantly wells up like the noise of springwater
in my ear. Tree limbs rise and fall like ecstatic arms.
Leaf sounds talk together like poets
making fresh metaphors.

The green felt cover slips;
we get a flash of the mirror underneath.

The conventional opinion of this poetry
is that it shows great optimism for the future.
But Father Reason says, No need to announce the future.

This *now* is it. Your deepest need and desire
is satisfied by *this* moment's energy
here in your hand.

## JUNE 9

*The Inner Workings*

The inner working of a human being
is a jungle. Sometimes wolves
dominate. Sometimes wild hogs.

Be wary when you breathe.
At one moment gentle, generous qualities,
like Joseph's, pass from one nature
to another. The next moment
vicious qualities move in hidden ways.

In every instant a new species rises
in the chest—now a demon, now an angel,
now a wild animal, now a human friend.

There are also those in this amazing jungle
who can absorb you into their own surrender.

If you have to stalk and steal something,
steal from them.

### *Stranded Somewhere*

If you are the body, that one is the soul
of the universe. If you are the soul,
that one is the soul within all souls.

Wherever you go, whatever you are, listen for the voice
that asks, Who will be sacrificed tonight?

Jump up then and volunteer. Accept
the cup that is offered every second.

If you are bored and contemptuous,
love is a walk in a meadow.
If you are stranded somewhere,
love is an Arabian horse.

The ocean feeds *itself* to its fish.
If you are an ocean fish, why bother
with bread the ground grows?

These jars of grief and trouble
that we call bodies, throw stones and break them.

My cage is this longing for Shams.
Be my worst enemy. Shatter it.

## Morning Wind

The morning wind spreads its fresh smell.
We must get up to take that in,
that wind that lets us live.
Breathe, before it's gone.

# JUNE 12

### *Lamp after Lamp*

You that prefer, as crows do,
winter's chill and the empty limbs,
notice now this that fills
with new leaves and roses opening
and the nightbird's song.

Let your love dissolve also
into this season's moment,
or when it's over you will buy
lamp after lamp to find it.

*Beyond Love Stories (1)*

Love comes with a knife,
not some shy question,
and not with fears for its reputation.

I say these things disinterestedly.
Accept them in kind.

Love is a madman,
working his wild schemes,
tearing off his clothes,
drinking poison, and now quietly
choosing annihilation.

A tiny spider tries to wrap
an enormous wasp. Think of the spiderweb
woven across the cave where Muhammed slept.

There are love stories,
and there is obliteration into love.

You have been walking the ocean's edge,
holding up your robes to keep them dry.

You must dive deeper under,
a thousand times deeper.

### Beyond Love Stories (2)

Love flows down. The ground
submits to the sky and suffers what comes.

Is the ground worse for giving in like that?
Do not put blankets over the drum.
Open completely.

Let your spirit ear listen
to the green dome's passionate murmur.

Let the cords of your robe be untied.
Shiver in this new love
beyond all above and below.

The sun rises,
but which way does the night go?

I have no more words.
Let the soul speak
with the silent articulation of a face.

## JUNE 15

*The Wide Plain of Death*

I placed one foot on the wide plain
of death, and some grand immensity
sounded on the emptiness.

I have felt nothing ever
like the wild wonder of that moment.

### Cuisine and Sex

You risk your life to feed desires,
yet you give your soul only short grazing spans,
and those grudgingly.

You borrow ten and repay fourteen.
Most of your decisions can be traced back
to cuisine and sex.

The fuel basket goes from one stokehole
to the next. Six friends hoist
your handsomeness and carry it
to the cemetery.

Food changes going from table to latrine.
You live between deaths,
thinking this is right enough.

Close these eyes to open the other.
Let the center brighten your sight.

### *The King Inside*

There are people with their eyes open
whose hearts are shut. What do they see? Matter.

But someone whose love is alert,
even if the eyes go to sleep,
he or she will be waking up thousands of others.

If you are not one of those light-filled lovers,
restrain your desire-body's intensity.
Put limits on how much you eat
and how long you lie down.

But if you are awake here in the chest,
sleep long and soundly.
Your spirit will be out roaming and working,
even on the seventh level.
Muhammed says, I close my eyes and rest in sleep,
but my love never needs to rest.

The guard at the gate drowses.
The king stays awake. You have a king inside
who listens for what delights the soul.

That king's wakefulness
cannot be described in a poem.

### Singing

When the soul first put on the body's shirt,
the ocean lifted up all its gifts.

When love first tasted the lips
of being human, it started singing.

----

### *Messengers from the Mystery*

Love is the way
messengers from the mystery
tell us things.

Love is the mother.
We are her children.

She shines inside us,
visible-invisible, as we trust
or lose trust,
or feel it start to grow again.

### *Dhu'l-Nun's Instructive Madness*

Some friends of Dhu'l-Nun, the Egyptian,
go to see him. They have heard
that he has gone spectacularly insane,
that he is a wildfire no one can contain,
this man who has been such a source of wisdom.
They arrive at his house. He yells out,
Hey, you had better watch out,
coming here. Who are you?

Don't you remember us? We are your friends.
What secret are you hiding with this madness?

Dhu'l-Nun begins to rave a mixture of filthy language
and gibberish. He rushes out and grabs up stones
and throws them at the group. They run.

See, he calls. You are not friends.
A friend does not run from pain
inflicted by a friend.

There is a joy within suffering
that is the kernel of friendship.
A friend is pure gold singing
inside the refining fire. He thrives on fights
and misunderstandings and even madness.

---

### *What the Friend Wants Done*

One who does what the Friend wants done
will never need a friend.

There is a bankruptcy that is pure gain.
The moon stays bright
when it does not avoid the night.

A rose's rarest essence
lives in the thorn.

### *Behind Each Eye*

Spring overall. But inside us
there is another unity.

Behind each eye
one glowing weather.

Every forest branch moves differently
in the breeze, but as they sway,
they connect at the roots.

### *The Verge of Tears*

You make our souls tasty like rose marmalade.
You cause us to fall flat on the ground
like the shadow of a cypress still growing at its tip.

Rainwater through a mountain forest,
we run after you in different ways.
We live like the verge of tears
inside your eyes. Don't cry.

You trick some people with gold ropes.
You tie them up and leave them.
Others you pull near at dawn.
You are the one within every attraction.

All silence. You are not alone, never that.
But you must at times become distracted,
because look, you have taken the food
that you were going to give to Jesus,
you have taken that out to the stable
and put it down in front of the donkey.

---

### *Inside This River*

Inside this river there is a moon
which is not a reflection.

From the river bottom the moon speaks.
I travel in continuous conversation
with the river as it goes.

Whatever is above
and seemingly outside this river
is actually in it.

Merge with it, in here or out there,
as you please.

This is the river of rivers
and the beautiful silence of endless talking.

## *The Miracle-Signs*

Here are the miracle-signs you want,
that you cry through the night
and get up at dawn asking,

that in the absence of what you ask for,
your day gets dark, your neck thin
as a spindle, that what you give away
is all you own, that you sacrifice belongings,
sleep, health, your head,

that you often sit down in a fire like aloeswood
and often go out to meet a blade
like a battered helmet.

When acts of helplessness become habitual,
those are the signs.

Excuse my wandering.
How can one be orderly with this?

It is like counting leaves in a garden,
along with the song-notes of partridges
and crows. Sometimes organization
and computation become absurd.

### The Self We Share

Look fish, you are already in the ocean.
Just swimming there makes you friends with glory.

What are these grudges about?
You are Benjamin.
Joseph has put a gold cup in your grain sack
and accused you of being a thief.

Now he draws you aside and says,
You are my brother. I am a prayer. You are the *Amen*.

We move in eternal regions,
yet we worry about property here.

Let this be the prayer of each:

*You are the source of my life.*
*You bring rivers from the mountain springs.*
*You brighten my eyes.*

*The wine you offer takes me out of myself*
*into the self we share.*

*Doing that is religion.*

### *An Invisible Bee*

Look how desire has changed in you,
how light and colorless it is,
with the world growing new marvels
because of your changing.

Your soul has become an invisible bee.
We don't see it working,
but there's the full honeycomb.

Your body's height, six feet or so,
but your soul rises through nine levels of sky.

A barrel corked with earth
and a raw wooden spile
keeps the oldest vineyard's wine inside.

When I see you,
it is not so much your physical form,
but the company of two riders,
your pure-fire devotion and your love
for the one who teaches you.

Then the sun and moon on foot behind those.

### The Bright Core of Failure

Sometimes you enter the heart.
Sometimes you are born from the soul.
Sometimes you weep a song of separation.
It is all the same glory.

You live in beautiful forms,
and you are the energy that breaks form.
All light, neither this nor that.

Human beings go places on foot.
Angels, with wings.

Even if they find nothing but ruins
and failure, you are the bright core of that.

## A Great Rose Tree

This is the day and the year of the rose.
The whole garden is opening with laughter.
Iris whispering to cypress.

The rose is the joy of meeting someone.
The rose is a world imagination
cannot imagine, a messenger
from the orchard where the soul lives.

A small seed that points
to the great rose tree.

Hold its hand and walk like a child.
A rose is what grows from the work
the prophets do, full moon, new moon.

Accept the invitation spring extends,
four birds flying toward a master.

A rose is all these and the silence
that closes and sits in the shade, a bud.

### *The Doctor Who Comes*

In his dream an old man appeared.
Good king, I have news.

Tomorrow a stranger will come. I have sent him.
He is a physician you can trust.
Listen to him.

As dawn rose, the king was sitting
in the belvedere on his roof.
He saw someone coming, a person like the dawn.
He ran to meet this guest. Like swimmers
who love the water, their souls knit together
without being sewn, no seam.

The king opened his arms
and held the saintly doctor to him.
He led him to the head table.

At last I have found what patience can bring.
This one whose face answers any question,
who simply by looking can loosen
the knot of intellectual discussion.

Now Husam touches my arm.
He wants me to say more about Shams.

# JULY

### *Stingy Aloeswood*

Fear and hurt are lassoes
drawing you through a door.

Lord, Lord, you say weeping.
Green herbs sprout where those tears fall.

Dawn comes; blindness drains away.
Each day is eternity.

Do not avoid your suffering.
Plunge it into the Nile.

Purify your stubbornness.
Drown it. Burn it.

Your body is a stingy piece of aloeswood
that will not let go its healing power
until you put it in the fire.

Now Shams leans near to remind me,
*That's enough sourness. No more vinegar.*

---

### *The Treasure's Nearness*

A man searching for spirit-treasure
cannot find it, so he is praying.

A voice inside says, You were given
the intuition to shoot an arrow
and then to dig where it landed,
but you shot with all your archery skill.

You were told to draw the bow
with only a fraction of your ability.

What you are looking for
is nearer than the big vein
on your neck. Let the arrow drop.

Do not exhaust yourself
like the philosophers who strain to shoot
the high arcs of their thought-arrows.

The more skill you use,
the farther you will be
from what your deepest love wants.

# JULY 3

### *Surrender*

Joseph is back.
And if you don't feel in yourself
the freshness of Joseph,
be Jacob.

Weep, and then smile.
Do not pretend to know something
you have not experienced.

There is a necessary dying,
and then Jesus is breathing again.

Very little grows on jagged rock.
Be ground. Be crumbled,
so wildflowers will come up
where you are.

You have been stony for too many years.
Try something different. Surrender.

## One Song

Every war and every conflict
between human beings has happened
because of some disaggreement about *names*.

It is such an unnecessary foolishness,
because just beyond the arguing
there is a long table of companionship
set and waiting for us to sit down.

What is praised is one, so the praise is one too,
many jugs being poured into a huge basin.
All religions, all this singing, one song.

The differences are just illusion and vanity.
Sunlight looks a little different
on this wall than it does on that wall
and a lot different on this other one,
but it is still one light.

We have borrowed these clothes,
these time-and-space personalites,
from a light, and when we praise,
we are pouring them back in.

### The Tree of Awe

How does part of the world leave the world?
How can wetness leave water?

Don't try to put out a fire by throwing on
more fire. Don't wash a wound with blood.

No matter how fast you run, your shadow
more than keeps up. Sometimes it's in front.
Only full, overhead sun diminishes your shadow.

But that shadow has been serving you.
What hurts you blesses you.

Darkness is your candle.
Your boundaries are your quest.

I can explain this, but it would break the glass cover
on your heart, and there is no fixing that.

You must have shadow and light source both.
Listen, and lay your head under the tree of awe.

When from that tree, feathers and wings
sprout on your soul, be quieter than a dove.
Don't open your mouth for even a *cooooo*.

## JULY 6

*Emptiness*

Now I return to the text,

> *And He is with you,*
> *wherever you are.*
>> (Qur'an 57:4)

But when have I ever left it?

Ignorance is God's prison.
Knowing is God's palace.

We sleep in God's unconsciousness.
We wake in God's open hand.

We weep God's rain.
We laugh God's lightning.

Fighting and peacefulness
both take place within God.

Who are we then
in this complicated world-tangle,
that is really just the single straight line
down at the beginning of ALLAH?

Nothing.
We are emptiness.

---

### *Birdsong from Inside the Egg*

There is an excess
in spiritual searching
that is profound ignorance.

Let that ignorance be our teacher.
The Friend breathes into one
who has no breath.

A deep silence revives the listening
and the speaking of those two
who meet on the riverbank.

Like the ground turning green in a spring wind,
like birdsong beginning inside the egg.

Like this universe coming into existence,
the lover wakes, and whirls
in a dancing joy,

then kneels down
in praise.

### *The City of Saba* (1)

In the city of Saba there is a glut of wealth.
Everyone has more than enough.
Even the bathstokers wear gold belts.

Huge grape clusters hang down on every street
and brush the faces of the citizens.
No one has to do anything.

You can balance an empty basket on your head,
and it will fill by itself
with overripe fruit dropping into it.

Stray dogs stray in lanes
full of thrown-out scraps with barely a notice.

The lean desert wolf gets indigestion
from the rich food. Everyone is
satiated with all the extra.

There are no robbers. There is no energy
for crime, or for gratitude.
And no one wonders about the unseen world.

### The City of Saba (2)

The people of Saba feel bored
with just the mention of prophecy.

They have no desire of any kind. Maybe some
idle curiosity about miracles, but that's it.

This over-richness is a sublte disease.
Those who have it are blind to what's wrong,
and deaf to anyone who points it out.

The city of Saba cannot be understood
from within itself, but there is a cure,
an individual medicine, not a social remedy.

Sit quietly and listen for a voice
that will say, *Be more silent*.

As that happens, your soul starts to revive.
Give up talking, and your positions of power.
Give up the excessive money.

Turn toward the teachers and the prophets
who do not live in Saba. They will help you
grow sweet again, and fragrant and wild and fresh,
and thankful for any small event.

### The Mystery of the Moment

To the mind there is such a thing as *news*,
whereas to the inner knowing, it is all
in the middle of its happening.

To doubters, this is a pain.
To believers, it's gospel.
To the lover and the visionary,
it is life as it's being lived.

*The Essence of Ritual*

Pray the prayer that is the essence
of every ritual. *God, I have no hope.*
*I am torn to shreds. You are my first,*
*my last and only refuge.*

Do not do daily prayers like a bird
pecking its head up and down.

Prayer is an egg.
Hatch out
the total helplessness inside.

## *Ramadan Silence*

When the Ramadan banner flies,
soul restrains nature, so it can taste its own food.

The strength of horses and the intensity of fire,
these are the powers of sacrifice.

Fasting, we honor the guest. Clouds of courage
give rain, because it was in this month
that the Qur'an rained down,
light through an opening.

Grab the rope, and be lifted out
of the body's pit.

Announce to Egypt that Joseph of Canaan
has come. Jesus dismounts the donkey,
and the sacrament table descends.

Wash your hands. Wash your face.
Do not eat or speak as you normally do.
Other food and other words will come in the silence.

*Hoofbeats*

The sound of hoofbeats leaving a monastery
where all is timed and measured.
You are that rider.

Someone who does not care very much about things
and results, illness and loss, you are the soul
inside the soul that is always traveling.

Mind gathers bait. Personality
carries a grudge. You weave cloth
like the moon leaving no trace on the road.

There is a learning community where the names of God
are talked about and memorized, and there is
another residence where meanings *live*.

You are on the way from here to there.
Your graceful manner gives color and fragrance
as creekwater animates the landscape it moves through.

The absolute unknowable appears as spring and disappears
in fall. Signs come, not the essence signified.

How long will you be a shepherd singlefiling us
in and out of the human barn. Will I ever see you
as you secretly are in silence?

*You Are as You Are*

You do not resemble anyone.
You are not the bride or the groom.

You do not fit in a house with anyone.
You have left the closed-in corner
where you lived. Domestic animals
get ridden to work. Not you.

You are as you are,
an indescribable message on the air.

### *Fierce Courtesy*

The connection to the Friend
is secret and very fragile.

The image of the Friendship
is in how you love,

the grace and the delicacy,
the subtle talking together
in full prostration, outside of time.

When you are there,
remember the fierce courtesy
of the one with you.

## *Who Says Words with My Mouth*

All day I think about it, then at night I say it.
Where did I come from, and what am I supposed to
    be doing?
I have no idea. My soul is from elsewhere,
I am sure of that, and I intend to end up there.

This drunkenness began in some other tavern.
When I get back around to that place, I'll be completely
sober. Meanwhile, I'm like a bird from another continent,
sitting in this aviary. The day is coming when I fly off,
but who is it now in my ear who hears my voice?
Who says words with my mouth?

Who looks out with my eyes? What is the soul?
I cannot stop asking. If I could taste one sip
of an answer, I could break out of this prison for drunks.
I didn't come here of my own accord,
and I can't leave that way.
Whoever brought me here will have to take me home.

This poetry. I never know what I'm going to say.
I don't plan it. When I'm outside the saying of it,
I get very quiet and rarely speak at all.

Shams Tabriz, if you would show your face
to me again, I could flee the imposition of this life.

### *The Oldest Thirst There Is*

Give us gladness that connects
with the Friend, a taste of the quick.

You that make a cypress strong
and jasmine jasmine.

Give us the inner listening
that is a way in itself
and the oldest thirst there is.

Do not measure it out with a cup.
I am a fish. You are the moon.

You cannot touch me, but your light
fills the ocean where I live.

JULY 18

### *Looking into the Creek*

The way the soul is with the senses
and the mind, is like a creek.

When desire-weeds grow thick,
your intelligence cannot flow,
and soul-creatures stay hidden.

But sometimes a flooding comes
that runs so strong
it clears the clogged stream,
as though with God's hand.

No longer weeping and frustrated,
your being grows as powerful
as your wantings were before.

Laughing and satisfied,
that masterful current
lets soul-creatures appear.

You look down,
and it's lucid dreaming.

The gates made of light
swing open. You see in.

---

### *Love for Certain Work*

Traveling is as refreshing for some
as staying at home is for others.

Solitude in a mountain place
fills with companionship for this one,
and weariness for that one.

This person loves being in charge
of the workings of a community.

This other one loves the ways
heated iron can be shaped with a hammer.

Each has been given a strong desire
for certain work, a love for those motions,
and all motion is love.

The way sticks and pieces of dead grass and leaves
shift about in the wind
and with the directions of rain and puddle-water
on the ground, those motions
are all following the love
they have been given.

### *People Want You to Be Happy*

People want you to be happy.
Don't keep serving them your pain.

If you could untie your wings
and free your soul of jealousy,

you and everyone around you
would fly up like doves.

# JULY 21

### *It's Afternoon*

Speak quietly
and say nothing that is not true.

It's afternoon. We need to be quiet
for a while. Speaking would be
such an orchard to walk in,
if we could do it without alphabet and sounds.

These stories and images and conversations
through which we try to show the inner life,
Husam and I,
they are like a donkey's head
that we carry from the skinning pit
to the kitchen. Let further changes come.

I give word-shape to this poetry.
Husam supplies the essence.

No, that's wrong. Both come from Husam,
*Ziya-Haqq*, the sun that is one
with earth and sky, one with intention and heart.

Husam, when my spirit completely recognizes yours,
they recall our being one.

### *Neither This nor That*

I may be clapping my hands,
but I do not belong to a crowd of clappers.
I am neither this nor that. I am not part of a group
that loves flute music, or one that loves gambling,
or one that loves drinking wine.

Those who live in time, descended from Adam,
made of earth and water, I am not part of that.

Do not listen to what I say as though these words
came from an inside and went to an outside.

Your faces are very beautiful, but they are wooden cages.
You had better run from me. My words are fire.

I have nothing to do with being famous,
or with making grand judgments or feeling shame.

I borrow nothing. I do not want anything
from anybody. I flow through all human beings.
Love is my only companion.

When union happens, my speech goes inward,
toward Shams. At that meeting
the secrets of language are no longer secret.

### *Betrayal into Trust*

When school and mosque and minaret
get torn down, then dervishes
can begin their community.

Not until faithfulness
turns to betrayal
and betrayal into trust
can any human being
become part of the truth.

*Mirror and Face*

We are the mirror as well as the face in it.
We are tasting the taste this minute
of eternity. We are pain
and what cures pain, both.

We are the sweet cold water
and the jar that pours.

*Sky-Circles*

The way of love is not
a subtle argument.

The door there
is devastation.

Birds make great sky-circles
of their freedom.
How do they learn that?

They fall, and falling,
they are given wings.

### *Fasting*

There is a hidden sweetness in the stomach's emptiness.
We are lutes, no more, no less. If the soundbox
is stuffed full of anything, no music comes.
But if brain and belly are burning clean
with fasting, every moment a new song
comes out of the fire.

The fog clears and new energy
makes you run up the steps in front of you.
Be emptier, and cry like reed instruments cry.
Emptier, write secrets with the reed pen.

When you are full of food and drink, an ugly metal
statue sits where your spirit should. When you fast,
good habits gather like friends who want to help.
Fasting is Solomon's ring. Don't give it
to some illusion and lose your power, but even if you have,
if you have lost all will and control,
they come back when you fast, like soldiers appearing
out of the ground, pennants flying above them.

A table descends to your tents, Jesus' table.
Expect to see it when you fast, this table spread
with other food, better than the broth of cabbages.

### *The Face*

So the frowning teacher came and left.
He is very consistent with that vinegar face.

But maybe he shows that to us and smiles with others.
Such a beautiful teacher, but so sour.
He is a pure standard for tartness.

Consider how your face is a source of light.
If you enter a grieving room
with the Friend in your eyes,
light will bloom there
according to the laws of sweet and sour.

Locked in a cell, you grow bitter, but out walking
in morning sunlight with friends,
how does that taste?

There *are* exceptions. Joseph caught the rose
fragrance down in his abandoned wellhole.

In this quietness now
I feel someone seated on my right
like a kindness that will never leave.

## *A Frog Deep in the Presence*

Since you have left, death draws us in.
A fish quivers on rough sand until its soul leaves.

For those of us still living, the grave
feels like an escape-hole back to the ocean.

This is no small thing, the pulling of a part
back into the whole. Muhammad used to weep
for his *native land*. To children who do not know
where they are from, Istanbul and Yemen
are similar. They want their nurses.

Stars go out to graze in the night sky pasture
in the same way that animals love the ground.

When I close my mouth, this poetry stops,
but a frog deep in the presence
cannot keep his mouth closed.
He breathes and the sound comes.

A mystic cannot hide his breathing light-burst.
I reach this point, and the pen breaks,
as Sinai once split open
for the generosity it was given.

### A Cleared Site

The presence rolling through again
clears the shelves and shuts down shops.

Friend of the soul, enemy of the soul,
why do you want mine?

*Bring tribute from the village.*
But the village is gone in your flood.

*That cleared site is what I want.*
*Live in the opening where there is no door*
*to hide behind. Be pure absence.*
*In that state everything is essential.*

The rest of this must be said in silence
because of the enormous difference
between light and the words
that try to say *light.*

*The Source of Joy*

No one knows
what makes the sould wake up so happy.

Myybe a dawn breeze has blown the veil
from the face of God.

A thousand new moons appear.
Roses open laughing.

Hearts become perfect rubies
like those from Badakshan.

The body turns entirely spirit.
Leaves become branches in this wind.

Why is it now so easy to surrender,
even for those already surrendered?

There is no answer to any of this.
No one knows the source of joy.

A poet breathes into a reed flute,
and the tip of every hair makes music.

Shams sails down clods of dirt from the roof,
and we take jobs as doorkeepers for him.

### The Soul's Friend

Listen to your essential self, the Friend.
*When you feel longing, be patient,*
*and also prudent, moderate with eating and drinking.*

*Be like a mountain in the wind.*
*Do you notice how little it moves?*

*There are sweet illusions that arrive*
*to lure you away. Make some excuse to them.*
I have indigestion, *or* I need to meet my cousin.

*You fish, the baited hook may be fifty*
*or even sixty gold pieces, but is it really worth*
*your freedom in the ocean?*

*When traveling, stay close to your bag.*
*I am the bag that holds what you love.*
You *can* be separated from me.

*Live carefully in the joy of this friendship.*
*Don't think,* But those others love me so.

*Some invitations sound like the fowler's whistle*
*to the quail, friendly,*
*but not quite how you remember*
*the call of your soul's Friend.*

# AUGUST

❧

### *Like Light over This Plain*

A moth flying into the flame
says with its wingfire, *Try this.*

The wick with its knotted neck broken
tells you the same. A candle as it diminishes explains,
*Gathering more and more is not the way.*
*Burn, become light and heat and help. Melt.*

The ocean sits in the sand letting its lap
fill with pearls and shells, then empty.
A bittersalt taste hums, *This.*

The rose purifies its face, drops the soft petals,
shows its thorn, and points.

Wine abandons thousands of famous names,
the vintage years and delightful bouquets,
to run wild and anonymous through your brain.

The flute closes its eyes and gives its lips
to Hamza's emptiness.

Everything begs with the silent rocks
for you to be flung out like light
over this plain, the presence of Shams.

# AUGUST 2

---

### Inside

Inside a lover's heart
there is another world,
and yet another.

*Sour, Doughy, Raw, and Numb*

If we are not together in the heart,
what's the point?

When body and soul are not dancing,
there is no pleasure in colorful clothing.

Why have cooking pans
if there is no food in the house?

In this world full of fresh bread,
amber, and musk, what are they
to someone with no sense of smell?

If you stay away from fire,
you will remain sour,
doughy, raw, and numb.

You may have lovely just-baked loaves
around you, but those friends cannot help.
You have to feel the oven fire yourself.

# AUGUST 4

---

## *This Overflow*

I could not have known what love is
if I had never felt this longing.

Anything done to excess
becomes boring except this overflow
that moves toward you.

*Value*

**Which is worth more**, a crowd of thousands,
or your own genuine solitude?
**Freedom, or** power over an entire nation?

**A little** while alone in your room
**will** prove more valuable than anything else
**that** could ever be given you.

## *The Great Untying*

We search this world for the great untying
of what was wed to us at birth
and gets undone at dying.

We sleep beside a stream, thirsty.
Cursed and unlucky his whole life,
an old man finishes up in a niche
of a ruin, inches from the treasure.

### *The Sacred Liquid*

Are you jealous of the ocean's generosity?
Why would you refuse to give
this gift to anyone?

Fish don't hold the sacred liquid in cups.
They swim the huge fluid freedom.

*Lion of the Heart*

You that come to birth and bring the mysteries,
your voice-thunder makes us very happy.

Roar, lion of the heart,
and tear me open.

## AUGUST 9

---

### *A Way of Passing Away*

There is a way of passing away
from the personal, a dying
that makes one plural, no longer single.

A gnat lights in the buttermilk
to become nourishment for many.

Your soul is like that, Husam.
Hundreds of thousands of impressions
from the invisible world are eagerly wanting
to come through you. I get dizzy with the abundance.

When life is this dear, it means the source
is pulling us. Freshness comes from there.

We are given the gift of continuously dying
and being resurrected, ocean within ocean.

*Out of Stillness*

I was happy enough to stay still
inside the pearl inside the shell,

but the hurricane of experience
lashed me out of hiding
and made me a wave moving into shore,

saying loudly the ocean's secret
as I went, and then, spent there,

I slept like fog against the cliff,
another stillness.

## *Our Caravan Bell*

Do you hear what the violin says
about longing? The same as the stick.
I *was once a green branch in the wind.*

We are all far from home.
Language is our caravan bell.

Do not stop anywhere.
The moment you are attracted to a place,
you grow bored with it.

Think of the big moves you have already made,
from a single cell to a human being.

Stay light-footed and keep moving.
Turkish, Arabic, Greek, any tongue
is a wind that was formerly water.

As a breeze carries the ocean inside it,
so within every sentence is,
*Return to the source.*

A moth does not avoid flame.
The king lives in the city.

*Light Building in the Pupil*

Birdcatcher, the birds you want are thirsty,
so you open the wine vat and let the fragrance draw us.
This is the wine the magi brought as a gift,
and the wine musk that led them.

There are certain night-wanderers
that you especially want. Not the drunkards,
and not the ones who just carry cups to others.

This is how it is to come near you.
A wave of light builds in the black pupil
of the eye. The old become young.

The opening lines of the Qur'an open still more.
Inside every human chest is a hand, but it has nothing
to write with. Love moves further in where
language turns to fresh cream on the tongue.

Every accident, and the essence of every being,
is a bud, a blanket
tucked into a cradle, a closed mouth.

All these buds will blossom.
In that moment you will know what your grief was,
and how the seed you planted has been miraculously
    growing.

### *The Circle*

Nothing is better than selling figs
to the fig seller. That's how this is.

Making a profit is not why we're here,
nor pleasure, nor even joy.

When someone is a goldsmith,
wherever he goes he asks for the goldsmith.

Wheat stays wheat right through the threshing.

How would the soul feel
in the beloved's river?

Like fish washed free and clean of fear.

You drive us away,
but we return like pigeons.

Shahabuddin Osmond joins the circle.
We will say this poem again
so he can play.

There is no end to anything round.

*The Polisher*

As everything changes overnight,
I praise the breaking of promises.

Whatever love wants, it gets,
not next year, *now.*

I swear by the one who never says *tomorrow,*
as the circle of the moon never agrees
to sell installments of light.
It gives all it has.

How do stories end?
Who shall explain them?

Every story is us. That is who we are,
from the beginning to no-matter-how-it-comes-out.

Those who know the taste of a meal
are those who sit at the table and eat.

Lover and friend are one being,
and separate beings too,
as the polisher melts in the mirror's face.

### *Gnostic Donkeys (1)*

I am a cup in the Friend's hand.
Look in my eyes. The one who holds me
is none of this, but this that is so filled
with images belongs to that one who is without form,

who knows what is best for a sandgrain
or a drop of water, who opens
and closes our ability to love.

We are being taught like a donkey.
A donkey thinks whoever brings hay is God.

In the same way, we are gnostics,
each with a unique experience
of what binds and what releases us.

We hear the voice of that and our ears
twitch like the donkey who hears his trainer.

Oats may be coming, and water!
What have you been given that is like that?

*Confinement*, you complain. Stick your head out.
That is all that will fit through
the five-sense opening.

### *Gnostic Donkeys* (2)

So. You have a wonderful view,
but no way *into* the prospect.

*I have no wings*, you mutter, depressed,
but this looking outside the senses
is a fire that kindles the body.

Small sticks and dry grasses catch
to a burning light, and here
is an odd bit: Even if not on fire
and shining, the sticks are *still* light.

To those who will come after, I say,
Life is not for waiting.

Do not postpone.
Love is bringing everyone by the ear
to a place where reason cannot go,
where Muhammed's eyes close in sleep,
and the night grows quiet.

Truth does not sleep. Sunlight does not go away.
The stars are suns. Shams is everywhere.

### *The Mystery of Presence*

The mystery of presence
will not arrive through the mind,
but do some physical work, and it comes clear.

An intellectual gets bound and wrapped
in complicated nets of connectedness.
Whereas the Friend rides the intelligence
that is creating genius at the center.

The mind is husk, and the appetites love coverings.
They look for them everywhere.
That which loves the kernel and the oil
inside the nut has no interest in shells.

Mind carries reams of reasons into court,
but universal awareness does not move a step
without some definite intuition.
One covers volumes of pages.
The other fills the horizon with light and color.

The value of scrip resides in gold
stored somewhere else. The value of a body
stems from the soul. The value of soul
derives from presence. Soul cannot live
without a connection there.

## The Arrow

There is a hand hidden in the pen's writing,
a rider invisible in a horse's dancing about.

We see the arrow's flight, but not the bow,
what is manifest, not the source.

But don't discard the arrow.
Notice the royal markings.

We are the confused polo ball
that does not see the bat's arc coming down.

A tailor tears out seams and sews again.
A blacksmith blows on the fire.

In one moment a saint forgets.
In another, a degenerate begins a forty-day fast.

## More Range

We are friends with the one who kills us,
who gives us to the ocean waves.

We love this death. Only ignorance says,
Put it off awhile, day after tomorrow.

Do not avoid the knife.
This friend only seems fierce,
bringing your soul more range,
perching your falcon on a cliff of the wind.

Jesus on his cross, Hallaj on his.
Those absurd executions hold a secret.

Cautious cynics claim they know
what they are doing every minute, and why.

Submit to love without thinking,
as the sun rose this morning
recklessly extinguishing
our star-candle minds.

*Inward Sky (1)*

You are the soul, the universe,
and what animates the universe.

I live and work inside you. I speak with
what was found in the ruins of a former self.

Concealed in your garden, I have become a ladder
propped against and leading up into the sky-dome.

Why cry for what is closer than voice?
I ask to hear the wisdom that uncovers the soul.

These four come with their answers.

> Fire: You have a saucepan to cook what's raw.
> > Wear it like a saddle on your back.

> Water: You have a spring inside.
> > Soak the earth.

> Jupiter in its goodluck aspect: Show your talent.
> > > Do something outside
> > > of time and space.

> Jupiter in its bad mood: Be consumed with jealousy.
> > What else is there?

## Inward Sky (2)

Prophets come and go for one reason, to say,

*Human beings, you have a great value*
*inside your form, a seed. Be led*
*by the rose inside the rose.*

Doubt is part of existence.
There is no proof of the soul.

So I ask in this talking with soul,
this prayer, this kindness, *When the soul*
*leaves my body, where will these poems be?*

Answer: It was like that in the beginning,
        so what are you worrying about?

Love, finish this ghazal, please.
You know which words will last.

Shams, say the meaning of the names,
the inward sky that you are.

*The Cat and the Meat* (1)

There was once a sneering wife
who ate all her husband brought home
and lied about it.

One day it was some lamb for a guest
who was to come. He had worked two hundred days
in order to buy that meat.

When he was away, his wife cooked a kabob
and ate it all, with wine.

The husband returns with his guest.
The cat has eaten the meat, she says.
Buy more, if you have any money left.

He asks a servant to bring the scales
and the cat. The cat weighs three pounds.
The meat was three pounds, one ounce.

If this is the cat, where is the meat?
If this is the meat, where is the cat?
Start looking for one or the other.

## The Cat and the Meat (2)

If you have a body, where is the spirit?
If you are spirit, what is the body?

This is not our problem to worry about.
Both are both. Corn is corn grain
and cornstalk. The divine butcher
cuts us a piece from the thigh
and a piece from the neck.

Invisible, visible, the world
does not work without both.

If you throw dust at someone's head,
nothing will happen.

If you throw water, nothing.
But combine them into a lump.

That marriage of water and earth
cracks open the head,
and afterward there are other marriages.

*The Breeze at Dawn*

The breeze at dawn has secrets to tell you.
       Don't go back to sleep.
You must ask for what you really want.
       Don't go back to sleep.
People are going back and forth across the **doorsill**
       where the two worlds touch.
The door is round and open.
       Don't go back to sleep.

### *On the Day I Die*

On the day I die,
when I am being carried toward the grave,
don't weep. Don't say, *He's gone. He's gone.*

Death has nothing to do with going away.
The sun sets and the moon sets,
but they're not gone.

Death is a coming together.
The tomb looks like a prison,
but it's really release into union.

The human seed goes down into the ground
like a bucket into the well where Joseph is.

It grows and comes up
full of some unimagined beauty.

Your mouth closes here
and immediately opens
with a shout of joy there.

*Longing*

Longing is the core of mystery.
Longing itself brings the cure.
The only rule is, *Suffer the pain.*

Your desire must be disciplined,
and what you want to happen
in time, sacrificed.

### *Whatever Gives Pleasure*

Whatever gives pleasure
is the fragrance of the Friend.

Whatever makes us wonder
comes from that light.

What is inside the ground
begins to sprout
because you spilled wine there.

What dies in autumn comes up in spring,
because this way of saying *no*
becomes in spring your praise-song, *yes*.

### The Death of Saladin

You left ground and sky weeping,
mind and soul full of grief.

No one can take your place in existence,
or in absence. Both mourn, the angels, the prophets,
and this sadness I feel has taken from me
the taste of language, so that I cannot say
the flavor of my being apart.

The roof of the *kingdom within* has collapsed.
When I say the word *you*, I mean a hundred universes.

Pouring grief water or secret dripping
in the heart, eyes in the head,
or eyes of the soul, I saw yesterday
that all these flow out to find you
when you're not here.

That bright firebird Saladin
went like an arrow,
and now the bow trembles and sobs.

If you know how to weep
for human beings, weep for Saladin.

### *Harsh Evidence*

What sort of person says that he or she
wants to be polished and pure,
then complains about being handled roughly?

Love is a lawsuit
where harsh evidence must be brought in.

To settle the case,
the judge must hear details.

You have heard that every buried treasure
has a snake guarding it.

Kiss the snake to discover the treasure.

### *You Are Most Handsome*

Think that you're gliding out
from the face of a cliff like an eagle.

Think that you're walking like a tiger walks
by himself in the forest.

You are most handsome when you are after food.
Spend less time with nightingales and peacocks.
One is just a voice, the other just a color.

### *Entering the Shell*

Love is *alive*,
and someone borne along by it is *more* alive
than lions roaring or men in their fierce courage.

Bandits ambush others on the road.
They get wealth, but they stay in one place.

Lovers keep moving, never the same,
not for a second.

What makes others grieve, they enjoy.
When they look angry, do not believe their faces.
It is like spring lightning, a joke before the rain.

They chew thorns thoughtfully,
along with pasture grass.
Gazelle and lioness having dinner.

Love is invisible except here, in us.
Sometimes I praise love. Sometimes love praises me.

Love, a little shell somewhere
on the ocean floor, opens its mouth.

*You* and *I* and *we*, those imaginary beings,
enter the shell as a single drop of water.

# SEPTEMBER

---

*We Three*

My love wanders the rooms, melodious,
flute notes, plucked wires,
full of a wine the magi drank
on the way to Bethlehem.

We are three. The moon comes
from its quiet corner, puts a pitcher
of water down in the center.
The circle of surface flames.

One of us kneels to kiss the threshold-dust.

One drinks with wine-flames playing over his face.

One watches the gathering
and says to any cold onlookers,

*This dance is the joy of existence.*

*Put This Design in Your Carpet* (1)

Spiritual experience is a modest woman
who looks lovingly at only one man.

It is a great river where ducks
live happily, and crows drown.

The visible bowl of form contains food
that is both nourishing and a source of heartburn.

There is an unseen presence we honor
that gives the gifts.

You are water. We are the millstone.
You are wind. We are dust blown up into shapes.
You are spirit. We're the opening and closing
of our hands. You are the clarity.
We are this language that tries to say it.
You are joy. We are all the different kinds of laughing.

---

### *Put This Design in Your Carpet (2)*

Any movement or sound is a profession of faith,
as the millstone grinding is explaining
how it believes in the river.
No metaphor can explain this,
but I cannot stop pointing to the beauty.

Every moment and place says,
*Put this design in your carpet.*

I want to be in such a passionate adoration
that my tent gets pitched against the sky.

Let the beloved come
and sit like a guard dog
in front of the tent.

When the ocean surges,
don't let me just hear it.
Let it splash inside my chest.

### *This Fish Way*

The ocean way is this fish way
of the watersouls of fish who die becoming the sea.
Fish do not wait patiently for water.

In this world full of shape,
there you are with no form.

You have made a universe
from a drop of my blood.

Now I am confused.
I cannot tell world from drop.
My mouth and this wine glass are one lip.

I am *Nobody*, the fool shepherd.
Where is my flock? What shepherd?

When I talk of you, there are no words.
Where could I put you, who will not fit
in the secret world, or in this one?

All I know of spirit is this love.
Do not call me a believer.
*Infidel* is better.

---

### *That Quick*

A lover looks at creekwater
and wants to be that quick to fall,
to kneel all the way down in full prostration.

A lover wants to die of his love
like a man with dropsy who knows
that water will kill him, but he cannot deny
his thirst. A lover loves death,
which is God's way of helping us evolve
from mineral to vegetable to animal,
each onward form incorporating the others.

Then the animal becomes Adam,
and the next stage will take us beyond
what we can imagine into the mystery
of *We are all returning*.

Do not fear death. Spill your jug into the river.
Your attributes will disappear,
but the essence moves on.

Your shame and fear are like felt layers
covering coldness. Throw them off
and rush naked into the joy of death.

# SEPTEMBER 6

*The Generations I Praise*

Yesterday the beauty of early dawn
came over me, and I wondered
who my heart would reach toward.
Then this morning again
and you. Who am I?

Wind and fire and watery ground
move me mightily because they are pregnant
with God. These are the early morning
generations I praise.

### *Something Opens Our Wings*

Something opens our wings. Something
makes boredom and hurt disappear.
Someone fills the cup in front of us.
We taste only sacredness.

### *Hunt Music*

Musk and amber remind us
of the air at sunrise,
when any small motion seems part
of some elaborate making.

The body's harp gets handed
to the soul to play.

The strings: rage, jealousy,
all the wantings mix their energy-music.

Who tuned this instrument?
Where wind is a string
and also Shams' eyes

reflecting a gazelle as it turns
to stalk the hunting lioness.

*No Better Love*

No better love than love with no object.
No more satisfying work
than work with no purpose.

If you could give up tricks and cleverness,
that would be the cleverest trick.

---

### The Origin of the World

Human beings seem to derive
from this planet, but essentially
we are the origin of the world.

A tiny gnat's outward form
flies about in pain and wanting,
while the gnat's inward nature
includes the entire galactic
whirling of the universe.

---

### *Dance*

Dance, when you're broken open.
Dance, if you've torn the bandage off.
Dance in the middle of the fighting.
Dance in your blood.
Dance, when you are perfectly free.

## SEPTEMBER 12

### *For Us This Day*

My soul keeps whispering, Quickly,
be a wandering dervish,
a salamander sitting in its homefire.

Walk about watching the burning
turn to roses. As this love-secret
we are both blasphemy and the core of Islam.

Do not wait. The open plain is better
than any closing door. Ravens love ruins
and cemetery trees. They cannot help but fly there.

But for us this day is friends sitting together
with silence shining in our faces.

### *Only the Best*

In the slaughterhouse of love
they kill only the best,
none of the weak or deformed.

Do not run away from this dying.
Whoever is not killed for love is dead meat.

*Sublime Generosity* (1)

I was dead, then alive.
Weeping, then laughing.

The power of love came into me,
and I became fierce like a lion,
then tender like the evening star.

He said, You are not mad enough.
You don't belong in this house.

I went wild and had to be tied up.
He said, Still not wild enough to stay with us.

I broke through another layer into joyfulness.
He said, It is not enough. I died.

He said, You are a clever little man
full of fantasy and doubting.

I plucked out my feathers and became a fool.
He said, Now you are the candle for this assembly.

But I'm no candle. Look. I'm scattered smoke.

### *Sublime Generosity* (2)

He said, You are the sheikh, the guide.
But I am not a teacher. I have no power.

He said, You already have wings.
I cannot give you wings.

But I wanted *his* wings.
I felt like some flightless chicken.

Then new events said to me,
Don't move. A sublime generosity
is coming toward you.

And old love said, Stay with me.
I said, I will.

You are the fountain of the sun's light.
I am a willow shadow on the ground.
You make my raggedness silky.

## Different Loads

Do not feed both sides of yourself equally.
The spirit and the body carry different loads
and require different attentions.

Too often we put saddlebags on Jesus,
and let the donkey run loose in the pasture.

Do not make the body do what the spirit does best,
and don't put a big load on the spirit
that the body could carry easily.

*Sheba's Hesitation*

Imagine that you are Sheba trying to decide
whether or not to go to Solomon.

You are haggling about how much to pay
for shoeing a donkey, when you could be seated
with one who is always in union with God,
who carries a beautiful garden inside himself.

You could be moving in a great circuit
without wings, nourished without eating,
sovereign without a throne.

No longer subject to fortune,
you could be luck itself,
if you would rise from sleep,
leave the market-arguing, and learn
that your own essence is your wealth.

### *Too Happy, You Could Not Sleep Last Night*

I am the slave who frees the master.
I teach the teacher.

I am essence born freshly every day.
I built the ancient civilizations.

I brush medicine on fading eyesight.
I relight intelligence.

In grief, I am pitchblack darkness.
On a feast day, the children's excitement.

I am the ground who fills the sky's brain
with fiery lightning-love, air, wind.

You could not sleep last night,
too happy with how I was remembering you.

No one is to blame that sometimes
I am a scandal, or obviously unfair.

The surface is rusting over.
I had better go into silence.

I am breathing too close
to this mirror's face.

### *Meadowsounds*

We have come again to that knee of seacoast
no ocean can reach.

Tie together all human intellects.
They will not stretch to here.

The sky bears its neck so beautifully,
but gets no kiss. Only a taste.

This is the food that everyone wants,
wandering the wilderness.
Please give us your manna and quail.

We are here again with the beloved. This air,
a shout. These meadowsounds, an astonishing myth.

We have come into the presence of the one
who was never apart from us. When someone chews
sugarcane, he is wanting this sweetness.

Inside this globe the soul roars like thunder.
And now silence, my strict tutor.

I will not try to talk about Shams.
Language cannot touch that presence.

### *Who Makes These Changes?*

Who makes these changes?
I shoot an arrow right.
It lands left.
I ride after a deer
and find myself chased by a hog.
I plot to get what I want
and end up in prison.
I dig pits to trap others
and fall in.

I should be suspicious
of what I want.

## Deliberation (1)

A friend remarks to the prophet, Why is it
I always make bad business deals?
It's like a spell. I become distracted
by business talk and get led into wrong decisions.

Muhammad replies, Stipulate with every transaction
that you need three days to make sure.

Deliberation is one of the qualities of God.
Throw a dog a bit of something.
He sniffs to see if he wants it.

Be that careful. Sniff with your wisdom-nose.
Get clear. Then decide.

The universe came into being *gradually*
over six days. God could have just commanded, *BE*.

Little by little a person reaches forty and fifty
and sixty and feels more complete.

God could have thrown full-blown prophets
flying through the cosmos in an instant.

Jesus said one word, and a dead man sat up,
but creation usually unfolds like calm breakers.

---

## *Deliberation* (2)

Constant slow movement teaches us
to keep working like a small creek
that stays clear, that does not stagnate,
but finds a way through numerous
details, deliberately.

Deliberation is born of joy
like a bird from an egg.

Birds do not resemble eggs.
Think how different the hatching out is.

A white leathery snake egg, a sparrow's egg,
a quince seed, an apple seed.
Very different things look similar at one stage.

These leaves, our bodily personalities,
seem identical, but the globe
of soul fruit we make,
each is elaborately
unique.

### *The Far Mosque*

The place that Solomon made to worship in,
called the Far Mosque, is not built of earth
and water and stone, but of intention and wisdom
and mystical conversation and compassionate action.

Every part of it is intelligent and responsive
to every other. The carpet bows to the broom.
The door knocker and the door swing together
like musicians. This heart sanctuary
*does* exist, though it cannot be described.

Solomon goes there every morning
and gives guidance with words,
with musical harmonies, and in actions,
which are the deepest teaching.
A prince is just a conceit,
until he does something with his generosity.

### *A Basket of Fresh Bread* (1)

If you want to learn theory,
talk with theoreticians. That way is oral.

When you learn a craft, practice it.
That learning comes through the hands.

If you want dervishhood, spiritual poverty,
and emptiness, you must be friends with a sheikh.
Talking about it, reading books, and doing practices
do not help. Soul receives from soul that knowing.

The mystery of spiritual emptiness
may be living in a pilgrim's heart,
but the knowing of it might not yet be his.

Wait for the illuminating openness,
as though your chest were filling with light.

Do not look for it outside yourself.
There is a milk fountain inside of you.
Do not walk around with an empty bucket.

You have a channel into the ocean,
yet you ask for water from a little pool.
Beg for the love-expansion.
The Qur'an says, *And He is with you.* (57:4)

## A Basket of Fresh Bread (2)

There is a basket of fresh bread on your head,
yet you go door to door asking for crusts.

Knock on the inner door. No other.
Sloshing knee-deep in clear streamwater,
you keep wanting a drink from other people's waterbags.

Water is everywhere around you,
but you see only barriers that keep you from water.

A horse is moving beneath the rider's thighs,
yet still he asks, Where is my horse?
Right there, under you. Yes, this is a horse,
but where's the horse? Can't you see? Yes,
I can see, but whoever saw such a horse?

Mad with thirst, he cannot drink from the stream
running so close by his face.

He is like a pearl on the deep bottom
wondering, inside the shell, Where is the ocean?

His mental questionings form the barrier.
His physical eyesight bandages his knowing.
Self-consciousness plugs his ears.
Stay bewildered in God and only that.

## SEPTEMBER 26

*Childhood Friends (1)*

A close childhood friend came once to visit Joseph.
They had shared all the secrets that children
tell each other when they are lying on their pillows
at night before they go to sleep. These two
were completely truthful with each other.

The friend asked, What was it like when you realized
that your brothers were jealous and what they planned to do?
I felt like a lion with a chain around his neck,
not degraded by the chain, and not complaining,
just waiting for my power to be recognized.

How about down in the well, and in prison,
how was it then? Like the moon when it is
getting smaller, yet knowing the fullness to come.
Like a seed pearl ground in the mortor for medicine
that knows it will now be the light in a human eye.

Like a wheat grain that breaks open in the ground,
then grows and gets harvested, then crushed
in the mill for flour, baked and then crushed again
between teeth to become a person's understanding.

Lost in love, like the songs the planters sing
the night after they sow the seed.

### *Childhood Friends* (2)

Then Joseph began questioning his friend,
What have you brought me? You know a traveler
should not arrive empty-handed at the door
of a friend like me. That is like going
to the grinding stone without your wheat.

God will ask at the resurrection, Did you bring me
a present? Did you think you wouldn't see me?

Joseph keeps teasing, Let's have it.
I want my gift.

The guest began, You cannot imagine
how I have looked for something for you.
Nothing seemed appropriate. You don't take gold
down into a goldmine, or a drop of water
to the Sea of Oman. Everything I thought of
was like bringing cumin seed to Kirmanshah
where cumin comes from. You have all seeds
in your barn. You even have my love
and my soul, so I cannot bring those.

I have brought you a mirror.
Look at yourself and remember me.

*Childhood Friends* (3)

He took the mirror from his robe
where he was hiding it.

What is the mirror of being? Non-being?
Always bring a mirror of non-existence as a gift.
Any other present is foolish.

Let the poor man look deep into generosity.
Let bread see a hungry man.
Let kindling behold a spark from the flint.

An empty mirror and your worst destructive habits,
when they are held up to each other, that is when
the real making begins. That's what art and crafting are.

A tailor needs a torn garment to practice his expertise.
The trunks of trees must be cut and cut again,
so they can be used for fine carpentry.
Your doctor must have a broken leg to doctor.
Your defects are the ways that glory gets manifested.

Whoever sees clearly what is diseased in himself
begins to gallop on the way. There is nothing worse
than thinking you are well enough. More than anything,
self-complacency blocks the workmanship.

*Childhood Friends (4)*

Put your vileness up to a mirror and weep.
Get that self-satisfaction flowing out of you.

Satan thought, I am better than Adam,
and that *better than* is still strongly in us.

Your streamwater may look clean,
but there is unstirred matter on the bottom.

Your guide can dig a side channel
that will drain that waste off.

Trust your wound to a teacher's surgery.
Flies collect on a wound. They cover it,
those flies of your self-protecting feelings,
your love for what you think is yours.

Let a teacher wave away the flies
and put a plaster on your wound.

Don't turn your head. Keep looking
at the bandaged place.

That is where the light enters you.
And don't believe for a moment
you are healing yourself.

## A Trace

You that give new life to this planet,
you that transcend logic, come.
I am only an arrow. Fill your bow with me
and let fly. Because of this love for you,
my bowl has fallen from the roof.
Put down a ladder and collect the pieces.

People ask, Which roof is your roof?
I answer, Wherever the soul came from
and wherever it goes back to at night,
my roof is in that direction.

From wherever spring arrives
to heal the ground, from wherever searching rises
in a human being. The looking itself is a trace
of what we are looking for.

But we have been more like the man
who sat on his donkey and asked the donkey where to go.

Be quiet now and wait. It may be the ocean one,
the one we want so to move into and become,
it may be that one wants us out here
on land a little longer
going our sundry roads to the shore.

*Rumi's birthday, in 1207.

# OCTOBER

❧

### *No Room for Form* (1)

On the night when you cross the street
from your shop and your house to the cemetery,

you will hear me hailing you from inside
the open grave, and you will realize
how we have always been together.

I am the clear consciousness-core
of your being, the same in ecstasy
as in self-hating fatigue.

That night, when you escape the fear of snakebite
and all irritation with the ants,
you will hear my familiar voice,
see the candle being lit,
smell the incense, the surprise meal
fixed by the lover inside all your other lovers.

This heart-tumult is my signal
to you igniting in the tomb.
So don't fuss with the shroud
and the graveyard road dust.

Those get ripped open and washed away
in the music of our finally meeting.

### *No Room for Form* (2)

And don't look for me in a human shape.
I am inside your looking. No room
for form with love this strong.

Beat the drum and let the poets speak.
This is a day of purification for those
who are already mature and initiated
into what love is.

No need to wait until we die.
There is more to want here than money
and being famous and bites of roasted meat.

Now, what shall we call this new sort of gazing-house
that has opened in our town where people sit
quietly and pour out their glancing
like light, like answering?

*Out Beyond*

Out beyond ideas of wrongdoing and rightdoing,
there is a field. I'll meet you there.

When the soul lies down in that grass,
the world is too full to talk about.

Ideas, language, even the phrase *each other*
doesn't make any sense.

### *This Dove Here*

Someone who does not run
toward the allure of love
walks a road where nothing lives.

But this dove here
senses the love-hawk floating above,
and waits, and will not be driven
or scared to safety.

*Hoping to Be More Alive*

You are an ocean in a drop of dew,
all the universes in a thin sack of blood.

What are these pleasures then,
these joys, these worlds
that you keep reaching for,
hoping they will make you more alive?

*Goldsmithing*

By Saladin's shop suddenly
I hear the music of gold
being hammered, gold and God.

As gold thins out,
the presence becomes a sheer
goldleaf light
on this goldbeater's face,
in his eyes as he works.

As the love-secret of Jacob
becomes Joseph's smile,
as lovers leave what keeps them confined,
as Job's patience dissolves to nothing,
you are the Friend
coming toward this touching.

You are the soul.
Be that, and when you hear yourself
in some hypocrisy,
cut free. Quickly, cut.

*This poem records the moment in Konya when Rumi
heard an inner music in the goldbeater's hammering coming
from his friend Saladin's shop. The legend is that he
began spontanously turning in the street in response to the
music of existence.*

*Water from Your Spring*

What was in that candle's light
that opened and consumed me so quickly?

Come back, my friend. The form of our love
is not a created form.

Nothing can help me but that beauty.
There was a dawn I remember
when my soul heard something from your soul.

I drank water from your spring
and felt the current take me.

## Walnuts

Philosophers have said that we love music
because it resembles the sphere-sounds of union.

We have been part of a harmony before,
so these moments of treble and bass
keep our remembering fresh.

Hearing the sound, we gather strength.
Love kindles with melody. Music feeds a lover
composure, and provides form for the imagination.
Music breathes on personal fire and makes it keener.

The waterhole is deep. A thirsty man climbs
a walnut tree growing next to the pool
and drops walnuts in one by one.

He listens carefully to the sound
as they hit and watches the bubbles.

A more rational man gives advice, You will regret
doing this. You are so far from the water
that by the time you get down to gather walnuts,
the water will have carried them away.

He replies, I am not here for walnuts.
I want the music they make when they hit.

### *Your Eyes*

I am so small I can barely be seen.
How can this great love be inside me?

*Look at your eyes. They are so small,
but they see enormous things.*

## In the Arc of Your Mallet

Don't go anywhere without me.
Let nothing happen in the sky apart from me,
or on the ground, in this world or that world,
without my being in its happening.

Vision, see nothing I don't see.
Language, say nothing.
The way the night knows itself with the moon,
be that with me. Be the rose
nearest to the thorn that I am.

I want to feel myself in you when you taste food,
in the arc of your mallet when you work,
when you visit friends, when you go
up on the roof by yourself at night.

There is nothing worse than to walk out along the street
without you. I don't know where I'm going.
You are the road and the knower of roads,
more than maps, more than love.

## *Love and I Talking*

Love says, You cannot deny me. Try.
I say, Yes, you appear out of nowhere
like the bubbles in wine, here and then not.

Love says, Prisoned in the body-jar,
singing at the banquet. I say,
This ecstasy is dangerous.

Love says, I sip the delicious day,
until night takes the cup away.
Then I insist night give it back.
The light I see by never changes.

The water of realization is the wine we mean,
where love is the liquid and your body the flagon.
Grace floods in. The wine's power
breaks the jar. It is happening now.

The water of waking becomes the one who pours,
the wine itself, and every presence at the banquet.
No metaphor can hold this truth that knows how
to keep secret and when to show itself.

### *What's Not Here*

I start out on this road,
call it *love* or *emptiness*.
I only know what's not here.

Resentment seeds, backscratching greed,
worrying about outcome, fear of people.

When a bird gets free,
it does not go back for remnants
left on the bottom of the cage.

Close by, I'm rain. Far off,
a cloud of fire. I seem restless,
but I am deeply at ease.

Branches tremble. The roots are still.
I am a universe in a handful of dirt,
whole when totally demolished.

Talk about *choices* does not apply to me.
While intelligence considers options,
I am somewhere lost in the wind.

# OCTOBER 13

## *I'm Not Saying This Right*

You bind me, and I tear away in a rage to open out
into air, a round brightness, a candlepoint,
all reason, all love.

This confusing joy, your doing,
this hangover, your tender thorn.

You turn to look, I turn.
I'm not saying this right.

I am a jailed crazy who ties up spirit-women.
I am Solomon.

What goes comes back. Come back.
We never left each other.

A disbeliever hides his disbelief,
but I will say his secret.

More and more awake, getting up at night,
spinning and falling with love for Shams.

### *Autumn Rose Elegy*

You have gone to the secret world.
Which way is it? You broke the cage and flew.

You heard the drum that calls you home.
You left this humiliating shelf, this disorienting
desert where we are given wrong directions.

What use now a crown?
You have become the sun.

No need for a belt.
You have slipped out of your waist.

I have heard that near the end
you were eyes looking at soul.
No looking now. You live inside the soul.

You are the strange autumn rose
that led the winter wind in by withering.

You are rain soaking everywhere
from cloud to ground.

No bother of talking. Flowing silence
and sweet sleep beside the Friend.

### *Medicine out of Pain*

In this drumbeat moment of red flowers opening
and grapes being crushed,
the soul and luminous clarity sit together.

All desire wants is a taste of you,
two small villages in a mountain valley
where everyone longs for presence.

We start to step up.
A step appears.

You say, I am more compassionate
than your mother and father.

I make medicine out of your pain.
From your chimney smoke I shape new constellations.

I tell everything, but I do not *say* it,
because, my friend, it is better
your secret be spoken by you.

## OCTOBER 16

### *The Moments You Have Lived*

As essence turns to ocean,
the particles glisten.

Watch how in this candleflame instant
blaze all the moments you have lived.

### *The Knots Untie* (1)

Fire is whispering a secret in smoke's ear,
This aloeswood loves me
because I help it live out its purpose.

With me it becomes fragrance,
and then disappears altogether.

The knots untie and open into absence,
as you do with me, my friend.

Eaten by flame, and smoked out into the sky.
This is most fortunate.

What's unlucky is *not* to change and disappear.
This way leads through humiliation and contempt.

### *The Knots Untie* (2)

We have tried the fullness of presence.
Now it's time for desolation.

Love is pulling us out by the ears to school.
Love wants us clean of resentment
and those impulses that misguide our souls.

We are asleep, but Khidr
keeps sprinkling water on our faces.
Love will tell us the rest of what
we need to know soon.

Then we'll be deeply asleep and profoundly awake
simultaneously, like cave companions.

---

*Looking for the Center*

The Friend comes into my body
looking for the center, unable
to find it, draws a blade,
strikes anywhere.

### *No Flag*

I used to want buyers for my words.
Now I wish someone would buy me away from words.

I have made a lot of charmingly profound images,
scenes with Abraham and Abraham's father, Azar,
who was famous for making icons.

I am so tired of what I have been doing.

Then one image without form came,
and I quit.

Look for someone else to tend the shop.
I am out of the image-making business.

Finally I know the freedom
of madness.

A random image arrives. I scream,
Get out! It disintegrates.

Only love.
Only the holder the flag fits into.
No flag.

### *Consider What Choices*

You wreck my shop and my house
and now my heart, but how can I run
from what gives me life?

I am weary of personal worrying,
in love with the art of madness.

Tear open my shame and show the mystery.
How much longer do I have to fret
with self-restraint and fear?

Friend, this is how it is.
We are fringe sewn inside
the lining of a robe.

Soon we will be loosened,
the binding threads torn out.

The beloved is a lion.
We are the lame deer in his paws.
Consider what choices we have.

## *Underwater in the Fountain*

When you die into the soul,
you lift the lid on the cooking pot.

You see the truth
of what you have been doing.

It looks terrible and sad
before the crossover move
that lets nine levels of ascension
turn into ordinary ground.

Into silence, a conversation with Khidr,
as there you are blind and deaf,
underwater in the fountain.

### *Silkworms*

The hurt you embrace
becomes joy.

Call it to your arms
where it can change.

A silkworm eating leaves
makes a cocoon.

Each of us weaves a chamber
of leaves and sticks.

Silkworms begin to truly exist
as they disappear inside that room.

Without legs, we fly.
When I stop speaking,

this poem will close,
and open its silent wings. . . .

### *Out in Empty Sky*

If you catch a fragrance of the unseen,
like that, you will not be able
to be contained.
You will be out in empty sky.

Any beauty the world has, any desire,
will easily be yours.

As you live deeper in the heart,
the mirror gets clearer and cleaner.

Shams of Tabriz realized God in himself.
When that happens,
you have no anxieties about losing anyone
or anything. You break the spells
that human difficulties cause.

Interpretations come, hundreds,
from all the religious symbols
and parables and prayers.

You know what they mean,
when the presence lives through you.

# OCTOBER 25

*What I See in Your Eyes*

Out of myself, but wanting to go beyond that
wanting what I see in your eyes,
not power, but to kiss the ground
with the dawn breeze for company,
wearing white pilgrim cloth.

I have a certain knowing.
Now I want sight.

### *The King's Lead-Camel*

There is a boy watching a cornfield,
keeping birds away by beating a small drum.

A king with a huge army camps nearby.
He has a tall and powerful camel
that carries big kettle drums and a drummer
at the front of his columns
constantly throbbing out courage
and determination.

That particular camel wanders
into the boy's cornfield.
The boy runs toward it
beating his toy tom-tom to scare it away.

A wise man advises, Don't bother, my son.
That camel is used to drumsound.
He will not scare.

So a lover completely given to the beloved
has no fear of death and no need of showing off.

It is with me as with the boy,
who stops beating his fear-drum
to watch and follow quietly
behind the king's lead camel
meandering through the corn.

### *I Am Not*

I am not the centuries-ago Muhammed.
I listen inside this day
like a fresh-fired Phoenix,
not some pigeon looking for seed.

There is a king for whom other kings
are stable boys. Some sip Hallaj's wine.
I drink his truth by the jar, by the barrel.

Qibla for the soul, kaaba for the heart.
I am the constant sky,
not a Friday mosque's ceiling dome.

Clean mirror, no rust.
I am the burning core of Mount Sinai,
not a mind full of hatred.

I taste a wine not pressed from grapes.
The one everyone calls to
when they are in sudden mortal danger,
I am That.

Gabriel could sit here beside me,
if he became God.

## *The Lord of All the East*

Slave, be aware that the Lord
of all the East is here.

A flickering stormcloud
shows his lightnings to you.

Your words are guesswork.
He speaks from experience.
There is a huge difference.

### *Judge a Moth by the Beauty of Its Candle*

You are the king's son.
Why do you close yourself up?
Become a lover.

Don't aspire to be a general
or a minister of state.

One is a boredom for you,
the other a disgrace.

You have been a picture on a bathhouse wall
long enough. No one recognizes you here, do they?

God's lion disguised as a human being.
I saw that and put down the book
I was studying, Hariri's *Maqamat*.

There is no early and late for us.
The only way to measure a lover
is by the grandeur of the beloved.

Judge a moth by the beauty of its candle.

Shams is invisible because he is inside sight.
He is the intelligent essence
of what is everywhere at once, seeing.

### *He Is a Letter*

Someone who goes with half a loaf of bread
to a small place that fits like a nest around him,
someone who wants no more,
who is not himself longed for
by anyone else.

He is a letter to everyone. You open it.
It says, *Live.*

### *Undressing*

Learn the alchemy true human beings know.
The moment you accept what troubles
you've been given, the door will open.

Welcome difficulty, as a familiar comrade.
Joke with torment brought by the Friend.

Sorrows are the rags of old clothes
and jackets that serve to cover,
and then are taken off.

That undressing,
and the naked body underneath,
is the sweetness that comes after grief.

# NOVEMBER

### *Birds Nesting Near the Coast*

Soul, if you want to learn secrets,
your heart must forget about shame
and dignity.

You are God's lover,
yet you worry what people are saying.

The rope belt the early Christians wore
to show who they were, throw it away.

Inside you are sweet beyond telling,
and the cathedral there,
so deeply tall.

Evening now, more your desire
than a woman's hair.

And not knowledge,
walk with those innocent of that,

faces inside fire, birds nesting
near the coast, earning their beauty,

servants to the ocean. There is a sun
within every person, the *you*
we call companion.

### *I Have Such a Teacher*

Last night my teacher taught me the lesson of poverty,
having nothing and wanting nothing.

I am a naked man standing inside a mine of rubies,
clothed in red silk.

I absorb the shining and now I see the ocean,
billions of simultaneous motions moving in me.

A circle of lovely, quiet people
becomes the ring on my finger.

Then wind, and the thunder of rain on the way.
I have such a teacher.

*Ashes, Wanderers*

In this battle we do not hold
a shield in front of us.

When we turn in *sama*,
we do not hear the flute or the tambourine.

Underneath these feet we become
*nazar*, the guide's glance,
ashes, wanderers,

as the moon diminishes,
until it is gone for a few days,
to come back changed.

Send for the planet Venus to play here.
Flute, drum, and strings are not enough.

No. Who but these musicians
could stand the heat that melts the sun?

*Move Within*

Keep walking, though there's no place to get to.
Don't try to see through the distances.
That's not for human beings. Move within,
but don't move the way fear makes you move.

### *A Lantern*

You so subtle you can can slip into my soul,
how would it be if you, for a time,
were living visibly here?

So hidden that you are hidden from hidden things,
you enter me, and my hiddenness
shines like a lantern.

You Solomon, who understands bird-language
and speaks it, what will you say now
through my mouth?

King whose bow no one can draw,
use me for an arrow.

Shams is the way I know God.

## *Unmarked Boxes*

Don't grieve. Anything you lose comes round
in another form. The child weaned from mother's milk
now drinks wine and honey mixed.

God's joy moves from unmarked box to unmarked box,
from cell to cell. As rainwater, down into flowerbed.
As roses, up from ground. Now it looks like
a plate of rice and fish, now a cliff
covered with vines, now a horse being saddled.
It hides within these, till one day it cracks them open.

Part of the self leaves the body when we sleep
and changes shape. You might say, Last night
I was a cypress tree, a small bed of tulips,
a field of grapevines. Then the phantasm goes away.
You are back in the room.
I don't want to make anyone fearful.
Here what's behind what I say.

*Tatatumtum tatum tatadum.* There is the light gold of wheat
in the sun and the gold of bread made from that wheat.
I have neither. I am only talking about them,
as a town in the desert looks up
at stars on a clear night.

*Love Dogs*

One night a man was crying *Allah. Allah.*
His lips grew sweet with the praising,
until a cynic said, So. I have heard you calling out,
but have you ever gotten any response?

The man had no answer for that.
He quit praying and fell into a confused sleep
where he dreamed he saw Khidr, the guide of souls,
in a thick green foliage.

Why did you stop praising? Because
I've never heard anything back.

This longing you express
is the return message.
The grief you cry out from
draws you toward union.
Your pure sadness that wants help
is the secret cup.

Listen to the moan of a dog for its master.
That whining is the connection.

There are love dogs no one knows the names of.
Give your life to be one of them.

# NOVEMBER 8

## *A Door*

I have lived on the lip
of insanity, wanting to know reasons,
knocking on a door. It opens.
I've been knocking from the inside.

### *Raw, Well-Cooked, and Burnt*

You ask, Why do you cry
with such sweetness all around?

I weep as I make the honey,
wearing the shirt of a bee,
and I refuse to share this suffering.

I play the sky's harp.
I curl around my treasure like a snake.

You say, What is this *I* business?
Friend, I've been a long time away from that.

What you see here is your own reflection.
I am still raw, and at the same time
well-cooked, and burnt to a crisp.

No one can tell if I'm laughing
or weeping. I wonder myself.
How can I be separated and yet in union?

## This Piece of Food

This piece of food cannot be eaten,
nor this bit of wisdom found by looking.

There is a secret core in everyone
not even Gabriel can know by trying to know.

*The Taste of Morning*

Time's knife slides from the sheath,
as a fish from where it swims.

Being closer and closer is the desire
of the body. Don't wish for union.

There is a closeness beyond that.
Why would God want a second God?

Fall in love in such a way
that it frees you from any connecting.

Love is the soul's light, the taste of morning,
no *me*, no *we*, no claim of *being*.

These words are the smoke the fire gives off
as it absolves its defects,
as eyes in silence, tears, face.

Love cannot be said.

*Inside the Rose (1)*

That camel there with its calf running behind it,
Sutur and Koshek, we are like them;
mothered and nursed
by where and whom we are from,
following our fates where they lead,

until we hear a drum begin,
grace entering our lives, a prayer of gratitude.

We feel the call of presence,
and the journey changes.

A dry field of stones turns soft and moist
as cheese. The mountain feels level under us.

Love becomes agile and quick,
and suddenly we are there.

This traveling is not done with the body.
God's secret takes form in *our loving*.

---

## *Inside the Rose (2)*

But there *are* those in bodies
who are pure soul. It can happen.

These messengers invite us to walk with them.
They say, You may feel happy enough where you are,
but we cannot do without you any longer. Please.

So we walk along inside the rose,
being pulled like the creeks and rivers are,
out from the town onto the plain.

My guide, my soul, your only sadness
is when I am not walking with you.

In deep silence, and with *some* exertion
to stay in your company,
I could save you a lot of trouble.

*Held Like This*

Held like this, to draw in milk,
no will, tasting clouds of milk,
never so content.

### An Edge of Foam

A dervish lover was told to turn
toward his own face,
and he did, saying, *Lord, lord,* for years
with no answer, no message back,
yet he was always there turning in silence,

with no music supporting him,
no tambourine rhythm.

A pigeon knows which roof to haunt.
Even if you drive it off,
it will circle and stay near.

This is the critical moment
when a swell of ocean turns
its edge to foam.

Every dervish has two mouths,
a crafted reed opening
and the lips of the fluteplayer.

Lord, don't speak from there.

# NOVEMBER 16

### *Whatever Circles*

Walk to the well.
Turn as the earth and the moon turn,
circling what they love.

Whatever circles comes from the center.

### *How Minds Most Want to Be*

You are the living marrow. The rest is hay.
Dead grass does not nourish a human being.
When you are not here, this desire we feel
has no traveling companion.

When the sun is gone, the soul's clarity fades.
There is nothing but idiocy and mistakes.
We are half-dead, inanimate, exhausted.

The way minds most want to be
is an ocean with a soul swimming in it.
No one can describe that.

My soul, you are a master, a Moses, a Jesus.
Why do I stay blind in your presence?
You are Joseph at the bottom of his well.
Constantly working, but you do not get paid,
because what you do seems trivial, like play.

Now silence. Unless these words fill
with nourishment from the unseen, they will stay empty.

Why would I serve my friends bowls
with no food in them?

*An Elephant in the Dark*

Some Hindus have an elephant to show.
No one here has ever seen an elephant.
They bring it at night to a dark room.

One by one, we go in the dark and come out
saying how we experience the animal.
One of us happens to touch the trunk.
A water-pipe kind of creature.

Another, the ear. A very strong, always moving
back and forth, fan-animal. Another, the leg.
I find it still, like a column on a temple.

Another touches the curved back.
A leathery throne. Another, the cleverest,
feels the tusk. A rounded sword made of porcelain.
He is proud of his description.

Each of us touches one place
and understands the whole in that way.
The palm and the fingers feeling in the dark
are how the senses explore the reality of the elephant.

If each of us held a candle there,
and if we went in together, we could see it.

### *I See My Beauty in You*

I see my beauty in you,
I become a mirror
that cannot close its eyes to your longing.

My eyes wet with yours in the early light.
My mind every moment giving birth,
always conceiving, always in the ninth month,
always the come-point.

How do I stand this?
We become these words we say,
a wailing sound moving out into the air.

These thousands of worlds that rise from nowhere,
how does your face contain them?

I am a fly in your honey, then closer,
a moth caught in the flame's allure,
then empty sky stretched out in homage.

*Grainy Taste*

Without a net, I catch a falcon
and release it to the sky,
hunting God.

This wine I drink today
was never held in a clay jar.

I love this world,
even as I hear the great wind
of leaving it rising,

for there is a grainy taste I prefer
to every idea of heaven:
human friendship.

### *This Recklessness*

I have no vocation but this,
and no need to touch every rose and thornpoint.

You are seeing though my eyes
and tasting with my tongue.

Why sell bitterness? Why *do* anything?
When you breakfast at the king's table,
there is no appetite for lunch.

I do not complain or brag about ascetic practices.
I would explain, but words will not help,
how there is nothing to grieve.

If you have no trace of this recklessness,
tell me your state.

I have forgotten how to say how I am.
The sun has already shone today.

Why should I describe the moon
coming up over our sleeping quarters?

*The Guest House*

This being human is a guest house.
Every morning a new arrival.

A joy, a depression, a meanness,
some momentary awareness comes
as an unexpected visitor.

Welcome and entertain them all.
Even if they are a crowd of sorrows,
who violently sweep your house
empty of its furniture,
still, treat each guest honorably.

He may be clearing you out
for some new delight.

The dark thought, the shame, the malice,
meet them at the door laughing,
and invite them in.

Be grateful for whoever comes,
because each has been sent
as a guide from beyond.

### *The Music*

For sixty years I have been forgetful,
every minute, but not for a second
has this flowing toward me stopped or slowed.
I deserve nothing. Today I recognize
that I am the guest the mystics talk about.
I play this living music for my host.
Everything today is for the host.

*Bonfire at Midnight*

A shout comes out of my room
where I've been cooped up.
After all my lust and dead living
I can still live with you.
You want me to.
You fix and bring me food.
You forget the way I've been.

The ocean moves and surges in the heat
of the middle of the day,
in the heat of this thought I'm having.
Why aren't all human resistances
burning up with this thought?

It is a drum and arms waving.
It is a bonfire at midnight on the top edge of a hill,
this meeting again with you.

### *When You Feel Your Lips*

When you feel your lips becoming infinite
and sweet, like the moon in a sky,
when you feel that spaciousness inside,
Shams of Tabriz will be there too.

*Empty*

When you are with everyone but me,
you are with no one.

When you are with no one but me,
you are with everyone.

Instead of being so bound up *with* everyone,
*be* everyone.

When you become that many,
you are nothing. Empty.

*Only Breath* (1)

Ah, true believers, what can I say?
I no longer know who I am.

     Not Christian or Jew or Muslim.
     Not Hindu, Buddhist, Sufi, or Zen.
     I am not from the East or the West,
     not out of ocean or up from ground.
     Not natural or ethereal, not composed
     of elements at all. I do not exist.

     I am not from China or India, not
     from the town of Bulghar on the Volga
     nor remote Arabian Saqsin. Not
     from either Iraq, between the rivers,
     or in western Persia. Not an entity
     in this world or the next. I did not
     descend from Adam and Eve or any origin
     story. My place is the placeless,
     a trace of the traceless, neither
     body or soul, I belong to the beloved,
     have seen the two worlds as one
     and that one call to and know,
     first, last, outer, inner, only
     that breath breathing human being.

*Only Breath* (2)

Friends, when I taste love's wine,
the two worlds combine,

and I have no purpose
but this play of presences.

If I spend one moment outside you,
I repent, and when I have

a moment of closer rapport,
I dance to rubble the ruins

of both. Shams Tabriz,
this friendship is all I say.

# NOVEMBER 29

### *Mary's Hiding*

Before these possessions you love
slip away, say what Mary said
when she was surprised by Gabriel.

*I'll hide inside God.*

Naked in her room
she saw a form of beauty
that could give her new life.

Like the sun coming up,
or a rose as it opens,
she leaped, as her habit was,
out of herself into the presence.

There was fire in the channel of her breath.
Light and majesty came.

I am smoke from that fire
and proof of its existence,
more than any external form.

### *Smoke*

Don't listen to anything I say.
I must enter the center of the fire.

Fire is my child, but I must be consumed
and become fire.

Why is there crackling and smoke?
Because the firewood and the flames
are talking to each other.

You are too dense. Go away.

You are too wavering.
I have solid form.

In the darkness those friends keep arguing.
Like a wanderer with no face.

Like the most powerful bird in existence
sitting on its perch, refusing to move.

# DECEMBER

*Awkward Comparisons*

This physical world has no two things alike.
Every comparison is awkwardly rough.

You can put a lion next to a man,
but the placing is hazardous to both.

Say the body is like this lamp.
It has to have a wick and oil, sleep and food.
If it doesn't get those, it will die,
and it is always burning those up, trying to die.

But where is the sun in this comparison?
It rises, and the lamp's light
mixes with the day.

Oneness, which is the true reality,
cannot be understood with lamp and sun images,
and the blurring of a plural into a unity is wrong.

No image can describe
what of our fathers and mothers,
our grandfathers and grandmothers, remains.

Language does not touch
the one who lives in both of us.

*The Sweet Taste of Grief*

I saw grief drinking a cup of sorrow
and called out,

   It tastes sweet, does it not?

You have caught me, grief answered,
and you have ruined my business.

How can I sell sorrow,

   when you know it's a blessing?

### A General Introductory Lecture

A nightingale flies nearer the roses.
A girl blushes. Pomegranates ripen.

Hallaj will be executed.
A man walks a mountain path, solitary
and full of prayer.

Narcissus at the edge, creekwater washing
tree roots. God is giving
a general introductory lecture.

We hear and read it everywhere,
in the field, through the branches.
We will never finish studying.

Neither of us has a penny,
yet we are walking the jeweler's bazaar
seriously considering making a purchase.

Or shall I say this with other metaphors?
A barn crowded with souls.
Quietness served around a table.

Two people talk along a road
that's paved with words.

### *Jars of Springwater*

Jars of springwater are not enough anymore.
Take us down to the river.

The face of peace, the sun itself.
No more the slippery, cloudlike moon.

Give us one clear morning after another,
and the one whose work remains unfinished,

who is our work as we diminish,
idle, though occupied, empty, and open.

---

*Your Face*

You may be planning departure,
as a human soul leaves the world
taking almost all its sweetness with it.

You saddle your horse. You must be going.
Remember that you have friends here
as faithful as the grass and the sky.

Have I failed you? Possibly you are angry.
But remember our nights of conversation,
the well work, yellow roses by the ocean,

the longing, the archangel Gabriel
saying, *So be it.*

Shams Tabriz, your face
is what every religion tries to remember.

### Listening (1)

What is the deep listening?
*Sama* is a greeting from the secret ones
inside the heart, a letter.

The branches of your intelligence
grow new leaves in the wind of this listening.

The body reaches a peace.
Rooster sound comes,
reminding you of your love for dawn.

The reed flute and the singer's lips.
The knack of how spirit breathes into us
becomes as simple and ordinary
as eating and drinking.

The dead rise with the pleasure of listening.
If someone cannot hear a trumpet melody,
sprinkle dirt on him and declare him dead.

*Listening (2)*

Listen, and feel the beauty of your separation,
the unsayable absence.

There is a moon inside every human being.
Learn to be companions with it.

Give more of your life to this listening.

As brightness is to time,
so you are to the one who talks
to the deep ear in your chest.

I should sell my tongue and buy a thousand ears
when that one steps near and begins to speak.

### *A Voice through the Door*

Sometimes you hear a voice through the door
calling you, as fish out of water
hear the waves, or a hunting falcon
hears the drum's *Come back. Come back.*

This turning toward what you deeply love
saves you. Read the book of your life,
which has been given you.

A voice comes to your soul saying,
*Lift your foot. Cross over.*

*Move into the emptiness*
*of question and answer and question.*

*Descend into the Pith*

Would you like to have revealed to you
the truth of the Friend?

Leave the rind,
and descend into the pith.

Fold within fold, the beloved
drowns in his own being. This world
is drenched with that drowning.

*Majesty and Helplessness*

Always check your inner state
with the lord of your heart.

Copper does not know it's copper,
until it is changing into gold.

Your loving does not know its majesty,
until it knows its helplessness.

## One Swaying Being

Love is not condescension, never that,
nor books, nor any marking on paper,
nor what people say of each other.

Love is a tree
with branches reaching into eternity
and roots set deep in eternity,
and no trunk.

Have you seen it? The mind cannot.
Your desiring cannot.

The longing you feel for this love
comes from inside you.

When you become the Friend,
your longing will be as the man in the ocean
who holds to a piece of wood.

Eventually, wood, man, and ocean
become one swaying being,
Shams Tabriz, the secret of God.

### A Dying Dog

A dog is dying on the road.
A man is weeping beside him. A beggar comes by.

Why the tears? This dog hunted game for me.
He kept watch at night.
Many times he drove away thieves.

What's wrong? Hunger has weakened him.
What's in the bag? Your food sack looks full.

Those are leftovers from last night.
I'll eat them later.
Give a little to the dog.

I give him these tears instead.
They are easier to come by.
Food on the road costs hard-earned money.

The beggar curses the man and leaves.
The beggar is right. The man's values are reversed.
Tears are worth more than money.
Tears are blood distilled into water.

Pay attention to those who want to change
so badly that they cry and dissolve
into lovingkindness and freedom.

## *The Nightwatchman (1)*

I sit by the side of one who watches
like the stars at night without sleeping watch.

My friend sits on the roof at night.
I attend that watching.

During the day I help with the gardening.
He is both a tender of flowers
and flowering trees.

It is no shame to be in this friendship,
or if it is, it is.

I was on my way elsewhere
when I saw the nightwatchman
sitting on the sky's roof like a guard.

Like a king, like a gardener in his garden,
rainwet stones, like the body's hand-me-down.

### *The Nightwatchman* (2)

The nightwatchman knows the way
from body to soul, how soul moves
in stomach bile, in blood and semen, in saliva.

Soul works inside those fluids
to keep the body fresh and full of energy.

So the stars and the planets and this world
are moving to bring grace here
through the cold night-clarity.

Events like battle arrows crisscross
from every direction. There is only one archer.

The skill of the sheepdog comes from the shepherd.
A city has a collective intelligence,
and each person there has a unique knowing.

Sometimes random bits pretend
to be a caravan, but it was a good messenger
who brought us the order out on the road
to *Come back. Come back.*

*Wean Yourself*

Little by little, wean yourself.
This is the gist of what I have to say.

From an embryo, whose nourishment comes in blood,
move to an infant drinking milk,
to a child on solid food,
to a searcher after wisdom,
to a hunter of more invisible game.

Think how it is to have a conversation with an embryo.
You might say, The world outside is vast and intricate.
There are wheatfields and mountain passes
and orchards in bloom.

At night there are millions of galaxies, and in sunlight
the beauty of friends dancing at a wedding.

You ask the embryo why he or she stays cooped up
in the dark with its eyes closed.

Listen to the answer.

*There is no "other world."*
*I only know what I have experienced.*
*You must be hallucinating.*

---

### *A Mouse and a Frog (1)*

A mouse and a frog meet every morning on the riverbank.
They sit in a nook of the ground and talk.

Each morning, the second they see each other,
they open easily, telling stories and dreams and secrets,
empty of any fear or suspicious holding-back.

To watch and listen to those two
is to understand how, as it is written,
sometimes when two beings come together,
Christ becomes visible.

The mouse starts laughing out a story he hasn't thought of
in five years, and the telling might take five years.

There is no blocking the speechflow-river-running-
all-carrying momentum that true intimacy is.

Bitterness doesn't have a chance with those two.
The God-messenger Khidr touches a roasted fish.
It leaps off the grill back into the water.

Friend sits by Friend, and the tablets appear.
They read the mysteries off each other's foreheads.

---

### A Mouse and a Frog (2)

But one day the mouse complains, There are times
when I want *sohbet*, and you're out in the water,
jumping around where you can't hear me.

We meet at this appointed time,
but the text says, *Lovers pray constantly.*

Once a day, once a week, five times an hour,
is not enough. Fish like we are
**need the** ocean around us.

Do camel bells say, Let's meet back here Thursday night?
Ridiculous. They jingle
**together** continuously,
talking while the camel walks.

Do you pay regular visits to yourself?
Don't argue or answer rationally.

Let us die,
and dying, reply.


\* *This is the night Rumi died, in* 1273.

### *What Is Love? Gratitude*

Don't unstring your bow.
I am your four-feathered arrow
that has not been used yet.

I am a strong knifeblade word,
not some *if* or *maybe*, dissolving in air.
I am sunlight slicing the dark.

Who made this night?
A forge deep in the earth-mud.

What is the body?
Endurance.

What is love?
Gratitude.

What is hidden in our chests?
Laughter.

What else?
Compassion.

Don't ask what love can make or do.
Look at the colors of the world.
The riverwater moving in all rivers at once.

*Tattooing in Qazwin (1)*

In Qazwin they have a custom of tattooing themselves
for good luck, with a blue ink,
on the back of the hand, the shoulder, wherever.

A certain man there goes to his barber
and asks to be given a powerful, heroic blue lion
on his shoulder blade.

And do it with flair. I have Leo Ascending.
I want plenty of blue.

But as soon as the needle starts pricking,
he howls, What are you doing?

The lion.

Which part did you start with?

I began with the tail.

Leave out the tail. That lion's rump
is in a bad place for me. It cuts off my wind.

The barber continues and immediately
the man yells out, Ooooooooooooooo, which part now?

*Tattooing in Qazwin (2)*

The ear.
Doc, let's do a lion with no ears this time.

The barber shakes his head and once more
the needle and once more, the wailing.
Where are you now?
The belly.
I like a lion without a belly.

The master lion-maker stands for a long time
with his fingers in his mouth.
Finally, he throws the needle down.
No one has ever asked me to do such a thing.
To create a lion without a tail or a head or a stomach.
God himself could not do it.

> Brother, stand the pain. Escape the poison
> of your impulses. The sky will bow to your beauty
> if you do. Learn to light the candle. Rise
> with the sun. That way a thorn expands to a rose.
> A particular glows with the universal.

> What is it to praise? Make yourself particles.
> What is it to know something of God?
> Burn inside that presence. Burn up.

## DECEMBER 21

### *A Star with No Name*

When a baby is taken from the wet nurse,
it easily forgets her and starts eating solid food.

Seeds feed awhile on the ground,
then lift up into the sun.

So you should taste filtered light
and work toward that which has no personal covering.

That's how you came here, like a star with no name.
Move in the night sky with those anonymous lights.

### What Jesus Runs From

The son of Mary, Jesus, hurries up a slope
  as though a wild animal were chasing him.
Someone following him asks, Where are you going?
  No one is after you. Are you the one
who says words over a dead person, so that
  he wakes up? *I am*. Who then could possibly
cause you to run like this? Jesus explains.

*I say the Great Name over the deaf and the blind,*
  *they are healed. Over a stony mountainside*
*and it tears its mantle down to the navel.*
  *But when I speak lovingly for hours with those*
*who take human warmth and mock it, when I say the Name*
  *to them, nothing happens. They remain rock,*
*or turn to sand. Other diseases are ways for mercy*
  *to enter, but this nonresponding breeds violence*
*and coldness toward God. I am fleeing from that. As*
  *little by little air steals water, so praise*
*dries up and evaporates with foolish people who refuse to*
  *change. Like cold stone you sit on, a cynic steals*
*body heat. He does not feel the sun.* Jesus was not running
  from anything. He was teaching in a new way.

*Cry Easily*

Keep your intelligence white-hot
and your grief glistening,
so your life will stay fresh.
Cry easily like a little child.

### *Soul, Heart, and Body One Morning*

There is a morning where presence
comes over you, and you sing
like a rooster in your earth-colored shape.

Your heart hears and, no longer frantic,
begins to dance. At that moment
soul reaches total emptiness.

Your heart becomes Mary, miraculously pregnant,
and body, like a two-day-old Jesus,
says wisdom words.

Now the heart turns to light,
and the body picks up the tempo.

Where Shams Tabriz walks, the footprints
are musical notes, and holes
you fall through into space.

## DECEMBER 25

*The Population of the World*

Christ is the population of the world,
and every object as well. There is no room
for hypocrisy. Why use bitter soup for healing,
when sweet water is everywhere?

## *Your True Life*

As you start to walk out on the way,
the way appears.

As you cease to be,
true life begins.

As you grow smaller,
this world cannot contain you.

You will be shown a being
that has no *you* in it.

*A Subtle Truth*

If you want money more than anything,
you will be bought and sold.

If you have a greed for food,
you will become a loaf of bread.

This is a subtle truth.
Whatever you love, you are.

*One Transparent Sky*

Lovers think they are looking for each other,
but there is only one search.

Wandering this world is wandering that,
both inside one transparent sky.
In here there is no dogma and no heresy.

The miracle of Jesus is himself,
not what he said or did about the future.
Forget the future. I would worship someone
who could do that.

On the way you may want to look back, or not,
but if you can say, *There is nothing ahead*,
there will be nothing there.

Stretch your arms and take hold
the cloth of your clothes with both hands.
The cure for pain is in the pain.

Good and bad are mixed. If you don't have both,
you do not belong with us.

When someone gets lost, is not here,
he must be inside us. There is no place like that
anywhere in the world.

*God in the Stew*

Is there a human mouth
that does not give out soul-sound?

Is there love, a drawing-together
of any kind, that is not sacred?

Every natural dog
sniffs God in the stew.

Look inside your mind.
Do you hear the crowd gathering?
Help coming, every second.
Still you cover your eyes with mud.

Wash your face.
Anyone who steps into an orchard,
walks inside the orchard keeper.

Millions of love-tents bloom on the plain.
A star in your chest says,
*None of this is outside you.*

Close your lips and let the maker of mouths
talk, the one who says, *things.*

# DECEMBER 30

### *Say Who I Am (1)*

I am dust particles in sunlight.
I am the round sun.

To the bits of dust I say, *Stay.*
To the sun, *Keep moving.*

I am morning mist,
and the breathing of evening.

I am wind in the top of a grove,
and surf on the cliff.

Mast, rudder, helmsman, and keel,
I am also the coral reef they founder on.

I am a tree with a trained parrot in its branches.
Silence, thought, and voice.

# DECEMBER 31

*Say Who I Am (2)*

The musical air coming through a flute,
a spark off a stone, a flickering in metal.

Both candle,
and the moth crazy around it.

Rose, and the nightingale
lost in the fragrance.

I am all orders of being, the circling galaxy,
the evolutionary intelligence,

the lift and the falling away.
What is and what isn't.

You who know Jelaluddin,
you the one in all,

say who I am.
Say I am you.

# AFTERWORD

## "AMERGIN'S SONG" AND
## WHAT MOVES THROUGH TIME

Robert Graves says in *The White Goddess* that the study of Western culture should begin not with *The Odyssey* or with *Genesis,* but with the ancient Celtic poem "Amergin's Song," a poem that was passed down in the oral tradition for almost three millenia until it began to be written down in various forms about 1100 A.D. It consists of a list of images that the poem's voice claims to inhabit. Amergin was the chief bard of the Milesians, a Celtic tribe of northern Spain. The legend is that he spoke this as his people were coming ashore on the southern coast of Ireland, around 1500 B.C. Amergin presents twenty-one images that announce the soul's shape-shifting presence. It is thought the poem may have a calendar embedded in it, and also an alphabet and a pantheon. Amergin means "born of song." I have freely reworked the poem from Robert Graves and his ideas, from Jean Markale, and several other sources. Maybe it truly *was* Beltane, May Day, 1530 B.C., that Amergin, with his right foot on land and his left in the surf, sang this into the Irish air.

### Amergin's Song

I am the stag with seven tines,
a flood widening across a plain.
I am wind in a trough of ocean,
the sun's tear, a globe of dew-wet
on an alder branch. I am a hawk
above the cliff, streaming and still,

a thorn beneath the thumbnail,
fire that makes a human head
of smoke above itself.

I am the oak and the lightning
that blackens one side, salmon swimming
and the taste of it cooked
on a hawthorne shaft, a hill of vineyards
and hazelnut trees where poets walk.

I am the charging wild boar, the ivy,
a breaker thrumming down its falling edge.
I am the infant under the unhewn dolmen stone,
flower in the midst of other flowers,
spearpoint. I am the bonfire on the hill,
the hive-queen and the shield,
the screech owl. I am the burning raft
with its body set adrift on nightwater.

The calendar within these images might be read like this: the royal stag with seven tines on each horn, fourteen total, stands as an emblem for late December, from the 26th through some days, on into January. The flood opening across a plain covers to mid-February; wind over deep water to mid-March.

The shining tear on an alder branch reflects the fragile first half of April. Hawk balancing over cliff edge, mid-May. A single flower among other flowers is for the moment ending June 9. June 10 to July 17 holds the midsummer inspiration in a boiling head of smoke over a bonfire.

The taste of salmon with poets walking a hillside of vineyards and hazelnut trees remains to the end of September. Then the fierce intent of the wild boar, ivy, and a ravening spearthrust runs through October. The threatening sound of winter ocean, the hive-queen of November, and a screech owl carry through December 20.

December 21, 22, and 23 enclose the silence of a hero buried in foetal position waiting for the new, the naked infant to be lain December 24 and 25 under the ceremonial standing stones like an opened cloth. Then, past midnight, the sea burial raft burns passage, and the stag is seen again on the steep mountainside. "Amergin's Song" presents these twenty-one glyphs for the psyche's motion through time. In a medieval copy of the poem, marginal glosses might name a human quality held in each image thus:

The sun enclosed in a drop of dew   —   for *clarity* and *grief*.
Hawk balanced in air   —   for *deftness* and *skill*.
Salmon   —   for *knowledge*.
Wild boar   —   for *the sudden veering of decision*.
A river flooding   —   for *expansiveness*.
The smoke-formed head   —   for *inspiration*.
The sound of winter surf, the hive, and the screech owl   —   for
    *death-fear* and *night-terror*.
Flower among other flowers   —   for *courtesy*.
The alpha stag   —   for *majesty* and *vigorous strength*.
Wind over ocean   —   for *depth*.
Thorn beneath thumbnail   —   for *betrayal*.
The poets' hill   —   for *the shared joy of making*.
Infant under a dolmen stone   —   for *revelation, grace,* and what
    we will never know, the *ignorance* and the *innocence*.
The burning funeral raft   —   a closing door, for *the approach of*
    *time's limit*.

Rumi has similar sequence poems about the everyday and extra-ordinary glory of the soul, our momentary, seasonal identities that are flickering and yet whole, wave and particle at once: "Say Who I Am," December 30–31; "Only Breath," November 28–29; "I Am Not," October 27; and "No Room for Form," October 1–2.

The Celts and the Sufis sing the same song about our inner indi-viduality, or almost the same. They praise the majesty of it, the vari-ety, the breadth, and the elusiveness.

Some may hear these poems as massively inflated, ego-giganti-cus bellowing. Whitman has been so misread. But Rumi's experi-ence is not inflation. Nor is Amergin's or Whitman's. What they hear and respond to is the double-music of being with nonbeing, crazy moth and candle, dazed bird inside invisible rose fragrance, Taoist and Tao merging. In their delerious lists these poems merge soul, spirit, body-intelligence, mind, beloved, and way into one voice. *This play of presences* is Rumi's province and provender, the dance floor, the dancers dancing, and the band. I would claim that such presences are at play in any attempt at creative making. It is what we do and are, artists or not. But enough grand theory. There truly is nothing *like* our lives, us in them, the open sky, and the world around. Nothing like. And these Celtic and Sufi poems that are mostly composed of a sequence of sentences beginning "I am . . . ," "I have been . . . ," or "I am not. . . ." are the expressions of what is so alive that it cannot be held for long with any sleight of language. Such poems delight in how identity is absorbed in the seasonal flow of being. They sense the sacredness of that ordinary immanence. I hear these poems as coming from the edge of an unknown. The trance poem that Amergin speaks is meant to free his tribe into the wild, into a multiple oneness. It comes from the essence of what it means to be a Celt, as Rumi's *I am, I am not* poems come from the core of what a Sufi is, a beyond-definition seeking. Both move out from the human heart as it searches for spirit, at risk and in danger, claiming an oceanic expansiveness. These extravagant poems sound familiar to us because we have heard many of our poets saying something similar—and particularly Whitman's *Song of Myself*, the entire fifty-two sections of which are an invitation to join him in his vast listening and his compassionate-identity witness.

I have enjoyed setting Rumi's imagery and visions to align with one whirling circle of the earth round the sun. Three hundred and sixty-six poetry glyphs put alongside the Gregorian numbering of our days. Sing, chronicity. Sing.

# REFERENCES

Each day entry reference has two parts:

1) Its location in Rumi's work. A pound sign followed by a numeral indicates the number of the rubai (short poem) or ghazal (longer poem) in Professor Furuzanfar's standard numbering in his edition, *Kulliyat-e Shams*, (8 volumes, Tehran: Amir Kabir Press, 1957–1966). These translations have been done in collaboration either with the Persian scholar John Moyne or with the work of the Cambridge Islamicist, A.J. Arberry. See the footnote on the first page of the Introduction for information on those books. A Roman numeral, I–VI, followed by numbers indicates the book and lines in the *Masnavi* of Reynold Nicholson's translation, *The Mathnawi of Jalaluddin Rumi* (London: Luzac, 1925–1940.) Nicholson was Arberry's teacher at Cambridge and a pioneer of Rumi transla- tion in English. The line numbers are approximate. ND refers to Nicholson's *Selected Poems from the Divani Shams-e Tabrizi* (Bethesda, MD: Ibex reprint, 2001). RO refers to Rudolf Otto, *Mysticism East and West* (New York: Meridian Books, 1957). PP refers to A.J. Arberry's *Persian Poems* (Everyman Library, 1954). "Arb." (Arberry) and a number and a letter indicate the page and the location on the page of a quatrain in A.J. Arberry's translation, *The Rubaiyat of Jalal al- din Rumi* (London: Emery Walker, 1949). No Furuzanfar numbers are available in that volume. Many of the *no ref.'s* indicate that the quatrain has been reworked from that collection. The notations beginning with "Ergin" refer to one of the twenty-two volumes of Nevit Ergin's translation (from Golpinarli's Turkish) of *The Shams* (the *Divani Shamsi Tabriz*) and to the ghazal numbers within that. The more puzzling Ergin references (Mag for his *Magnificent One* and GO for Golpinarli's *Gul Deste*) may be deciphered by referring to the more detailed References section at the back of *The Glance* (see below). A project is underway to discover and list the corresponding standard Furuzanfar numbers for Dr. Ergin's work, but that task is not yet complete. See the Web site at www.dar-al-masnavi.org/erg-foruz-concord.htlm. In several cases I was unable to find the reference. Bad bookkeeping. Whatever you call the collaborative effort at translation that I do, it is not scholarship. I aspire more to the soulbook practice described in the Introduction.

2) The second element in each reference entry locates it in one of the volumes of my translations. For *A Year With Rumi* some poems have been edited, relineated, re-titled, or excerpted. Readers can find the longer versions, the context, in the following books. These are their abbreviations in the reference listings: ER: *The Essential Rumi, New Expanded Edition* (HarperSanFrancisco, 2004). BoL: *Rumi, The Book of Love* (HarperSanFrancisco, 2003). SoR: *The Soul of Rumi* (HarperSanFranciso, 2001). SIAY: *Say I Am You* (Maypop, 1994). LT: *Like This* (Maypop, 1990). TL: *This Longing* (Threshold/Shambhala, 1988). UR: *Unseen Rain* (Threshold/Shambhala, 1986). WAT: *We Are Three* (Maypop, 1987). DL: *Delicious Laughter* (Maypop, 1990). OHBW: *One-Handed Basket Weaving* (Maypop, 1991). G: *The Glance* (Viking, 1999). B: *Birdsong* (Maypop, 1993). IR: *The Illuminated Rumi* (Broadway, 1997). Poems that appear here for the first time are indicated by AYWR.

## January

1 – V, 672ff; ER; 2 – I, 1489ff; ER; 3 – Arb. 145b; ER; 4 – #2336; ER; 5 – III, 3762ff; ER; 6 – Arb. 178a; ER; 7 – #825; ER; 8 – #2429; ER; 9 – III, 4624ff; ER; 10 – #831; ER; 11 – II, 2212ff; ER; 12 – #1299; ER; 13 – I, 2870ff; ER; 14 – #181; AYWR; 15 – IV, 1990ff; SIAY; 16 – #82; ER; 17 – Arb. 153b; ER; 18 – IV, 349ff; SoR; 19 – #1288; ER; 20 – V, 2020ff; ER; 21 – #170; ER; 22 – #388; ER; 23 – #2303; ER; 24 – III, 1972ff; ER; 25 – III, 1972ff; ER; 26 – III, 1972ff; ER; 27 – III, 1972ff; ER; 28 – IV, 2683ff; ER; 29 – IV, 490ff; SoR; 30 – V, 2143ff; ER; 31 – IV, 1960ff; ER

## February

1 — #1359; ER; 2 – no ref.; AYWR; 3 – #1047; ER; 4 – #617; ER; 5 – Arberry 66a; ER; 6 – #598; ER; 7 – #828; ER; 8 – II, 2214ff; ER; 9 – Discourse #4; SIAY; 10 – #185; SIAY; 11 – IV, 3226ff; SIAY; 12 – IV, 3628ff; ER; 13 – no ref.; BoL; 14 – no ref.; ER; 15 – #667; ER; 16 – IV, 2611ff; ER; 17 – IV, 2537ff; ER; 18 – #436; SIAY; 19 – #436; SIAY; 20 – no ref.; ER; 21 – #882; ER; 22 – I, 3325ff; ER; 23 – #36; ER; 24 – #1924; ER; 25 – #2779; ER; 26 – no ref.; IR; 27 – IV, 3678ff; ER; 28 – IV, 3708ff; ER; 29 – VI, 1466ff; OHBW

## March

1 – III, 4694ff; ER; 2 – #1888; ER; 3 – #1051; ER; 4 – #951; ER; 5 – #747; ER;
6 – VI, 216ff; ER; 7 – #612; ER; 8 – III, 1114ff; ER; 9 – II, preface; ER;
10 – #940; ER; 11 – #1025; ER; 12 – II, 156ff; ER; 13 – #7; ER; 14 – #1270; ER;
15 – Letters #20; TL; 16 – #397; ER; 17 – VI, 642ff; ER; 18 – #628; ER;
19 – #3019; ER; 20 – #393; ER; 21 – #2003; ER; 22 – #636; ER; 23 – #823; ER;
24 – #211; ER; 25 – #2805; ER; 26 – #914; ER; 27 – #2196; ER; 28 – #707;
SIAY; 29 – V, 183ff; ER; 30 – V, 183ff; ER; 31 – #569; ER

## April

1 – #2693; ER; 2 – #25; ER; 3 – V, 2221ff; ER; 4 – #12; ER; 5 – V, 3831ff; ER;
6 – no ref.; B; 7 – #2728; ER; 8 – II, 2338ff; ER; 9 – #2776; ER; 10 – no ref.;
SIAY; 11 – #532; LT; 12 – #1754; ER; 13 – IV, 3628ff; OHBW; 14 – Ergin 7a,
#76; G; 15 – no ref.; IR; 16 – #1635; ER; 17 – no ref.; ER; 18 – V, 2855; SIAY;
19 – IV, 863; SIAY; 20 – IV, 863; SIAY; 21 – no ref; SIAY; 22 – #2; ER; 23 – IV,
2921ff; SoR; 24 – no ref.; SoR; 25 – V, 1105ff; OHBW; 26 – VI, 2686ff; TL;
27 – IV, 2034ff; SoR; 28 – V, 420ff; ER; 29 – V, 420ff; ER; 30 – I, 30ff; ER

## May

1 – VI, 3914ff; OHBW; 2 – Ergin, no ref.; BoL; 3 – no ref.; 4 – Ergin 8b, #162;
SoR; 5 – II, 1932; ER; 6 – I, 2163ff; ER; 7 – Ergin 3, #159; G; 8 – #258; ER;
9 – VI, 3986ff; ER; 10 – no ref.; 11 – #7; ER; 12 – #730; ER; 13 – II, 1720ff; ER;
14 – #1195; LT; 15 – VI, 2195; ER; 16 – #3050; LT; 17 – IV, 2540ff; ER; 18 – IV,
2540ff; ER; 19 – #1246; ER; 20 – Arb.169b; B; 21 – Arb.12b; B; 22 – III, 3204ff;
DL; 23 – #723; ER; 24 – PP; ER; 25 – Ergin 7b, #223; G; 26 – II, 2580ff; ER;
27 – III, 3545ff; ER; 28 – #1447; ER; 29 – #1678; ER; 30 – #1972; ER; 31 – no
ref.; AYWR

## June

1 – Ergin 3, #117; SoR; 2 – III, 4258ff; SoR; 3 – #171; BoL; 4 – no ref.; BoL;
5 – #2028; ER; 6 – #2103; ER; 7 – #2120; ER; 8 – IV, 3259ff; ER; 9 – no ref.;
DL; 10 – no ref.; AYWR; 11 – #751; ER; 12 – no ref.; SoR; 13 – no ref.; SoR;

14 – no ref.; SoR; **15** – no ref.; SoR; **16** – Ergin 8a, #83; SoR; **17** – III, 1222ff;
ER; **18** – no ref.; B; **19** – no ref.; B; **20** – II, 1386ff; OHBW; **21** – no ref.; B;
**22** – no ref.; B; **23** – #1879; WAT; **24** – VI, 3220ff; WAT; **25** – II, 1680ff; WAT;
**26** – Ergin 7b, #256; G; **27** – Ergin 2, #93; G; **28** – Ergin 7b, #271; G;
**29** – Ergin 4, #66; G; **30** – I, 34ff; ER

*July*

**1** – #887; ER; **2** – VI, 2347ff; OHBW; **3** – I, 1878ff; OHBW; **4** – II, 3641ff, III,
2122ff; OHBW; **5** – #2155; LT; **6** – I, 1480; OHBW; **7** – III, 4664ff; OHBW;
**8** – III, 2656ff; OHBW; **9** – III, 2656ff; OHBW; **10** – IV, 3262ff; OHBW;
**11** – III, 2149ff; OHBW; **12** – #892; AYWR; **13** – Ergin 1, #143; **14** – Ergin 2,
#120; G; **15** – Ergin 4, #24; G; **16** – Safa anthology; ER; **17** – Ergin 76, #181; G;
**18** – III, 1824ff; ONBW; **19** – III, 1616ff; OHBW; **20** – no ref.; B; **21** – IV,
3818ff; SoR; **22** – #1615; LT; **23** – #611; SoR; **24** – #1652; ER; **25** – no ref.; B;
**26** – #1739; TL; **27** – Ergin 11, #52; AYWR; **28** – #2000; ER; **29** – #1925; ER;
**30** – #423; SoR; **31** – III, 212ff; SoR

*August*

**1** – Ergin 2, #79; G; **2** – Ergin 8a, #22; G; **3** – Ergin 8a, #25; SoR; **4** – #602;
SoR; **5** – no ref.; B; **6** – no ref.; B; **7** – no ref.; B; **8** – no ref.; B; **9** – V, 4204ff;
SIAY, **10** – no ref.; B; **11** – #304; SIAY; **12** – #2894; ER; **13** – no ref.; BoL;
**14** – no ref.; BoL; **15** – #477; AYWR; **16** – #477; AYWR; **17** – III, 2526ff; AYWR;
**18** – II, 1303ff; AYWR; **19** – no ref.; BoL; **20** – Ergin 7b, #235; AYWR;
**21** – Ergin 7b, #235; AYWR; **22** – V, 3409ff; WAT; **23** – V, 3409ff; WAT;
**24** – #91; ER; **25** – #911; LT; **26** – #191; SIAY; **27** – Ergin 8b, #135; **28** – Ergin
8b, #180; SoR; **29** – I, 4000ff; SoR; **30** – #1078; ER; **31** – Ergin 2, #38; G

*September*

**1** – #2395; WAT; **2** – V, 3292ff; DL; **3** – V, 3292ff; DL; **4** – Ergin 8b, #151; SoR;
**5** – III, 3884ff; SoR; **6** – Ergin 8a, #55; SoR; **7** – #1084; ER; **8** – Ergin 8a, #62;
SoR; **9** – #152; ER; **10** – IV, 3766ff; SoR; **11** – III,95ff; TL; **12** – no ref.; BoL;
**13** – #681; ER; **14** – #1373; LT; **15** – #1373; LT; **16** – V, 1080ff; OHBW; **17** – IV,
1082ff; ER; **18** – Arb.64a; ER; **19** – #3079; ER; **20** – VI, 3682ff; ER; **21** – III,
3494ff; WAT; **22** – III, 3494ff; WAT; **23** – IV, 475ff; ER; **24** – V, 1051ff; TL;

25 – V, 1051ff; TL; **26** – I, 3150; ER; **27** – I, 3150; ER; **28** – I, 3150; ER; **29** – I, 3150; ER; **30** – #100; SIAY

## October

1 – #1145, ER; **2** – #1145, ER; **3** – #158, ER; **4** – no ref.; B; **5** – no ref.; BoL;
**6** – Ergin 16, #139; AYWR; **7** – #1001; ER; **8** – IV, 745ff; SoR; **9** – #798; ER;
**10** – #2195; ER; **11** – III, 4735ff; ER; **12** – Ergin 2, #69; G; **13** – #2166; ER;
**14** – Ergin 9b, #223; G; **15** – #2259; ER; **16** – no ref.; B; **17** – Ergin 4, #52; G;
**18** – Ergin 4, #52; G; **19** – #167; ER; **20** – #2449; ER; **21** – no ref.; BoL;
**22** – Ergin 2, #80; G; **23** – Ergin Mag 45, HSg 59, v740ff; G; **24** – Ergin 2,
#103; G; **25** – Ergin 3, #111; G; **26** – III, 4089ff; ER; **27** – Ergin, unpub.;
AYWR; **28** – Arb. 19a; ER; **29** – #2627; ER; **30** – #494; ER; **31** – Ergin Mag,
HMM g284, v3864–69, 3873, g291, v3964, 3975, 3977; G

## November

1 – Ergin 2, #130; G; **2** – #2015, ER; **3** – Ergin 2, #111; G; **4** – #317; ER;
**5** – #2832; ER; **6** – #1937; ER; **7** – III, 189ff; ER; **8** – #1249; ER; **9** – Ergin
Mag,GD, 190; G; **10** – #79; ER; **11** – Ergin 2, #138; G; **12** – Ergin 4, #1; G;
**13** – Ergin 4, #1; G; **14** – #1125; ER; **15** – VI, 1983ff; ER; **16** – #318; ER;
**17** – #2987; ER; **18** – III, 1259ff; ER; **19** – Ergin 4, #93; G; **20** – Ergin 3, #27;
G; **21** – Ergin 2, #79; G; **22** – V, 3646ff; ER; **23** – I, 2084ff; ER; **24** – #2110; ER;
**25** – #807; ER; **26** – #1793; WAT; **27** – ND, #31; AYWR; **28** – ND, #31; AYWR;
**29** – III, 3700ff; OHBW; **30** – no ref.; BoL

## December

1 – III, 3669ff; OHBW; **2** – no ref.; B; **3** – Ergin 4, #45; G; **4** – Ergin 4, ghazal
#, v2390; G; **5** – #2283; ER; **6** – Ergin 7b, #181; G; **7** – Ergin 7b, #181; **8** – Ergin
7b, #161; G; **9** – no ref.; B; **10** – no ref.; BoL; **11** – Ergin 8a, #31; SoR; **12** – V,
477ff; ER; **13** – Ergin 16, #140; AYWR; **14** – Ergin 16, #140; AYWR; **15** – III,
49ff; WAT; **16** – V, 2632ff; TL; **17** – V, 2632ff; **18** – #1126; LT; **19** – I, 2981ff; DL;
**20** – I, 2981ff; **21** – III, 1284ff; SoR; **22** – III, 2570ff; ER; **23** – V, 1ff; DL;
**24** – no ref.; BoL; **25** – #1091; ER; **26** – #153; UR; **27** – no ref.; B; **28** – #425;
ER; **29** – Ergin 7a, #105; G; **30** – RO, 93; SIAY; **31** – RO,93

# Index of Titles